The geographical scope of this book is defined as Ukraine plus the western side o[...]
St.Petersburg and north to Arkhangelsk and Murmansk, plus the Baltic states of Lat[...] [...]onia and Lithuania. The Republic of Georgia, lying at the intersection of Eastern Europe and Western Asia, which shares the Black Sea coastline with Ukraine, Russia and other nations, is also covered.

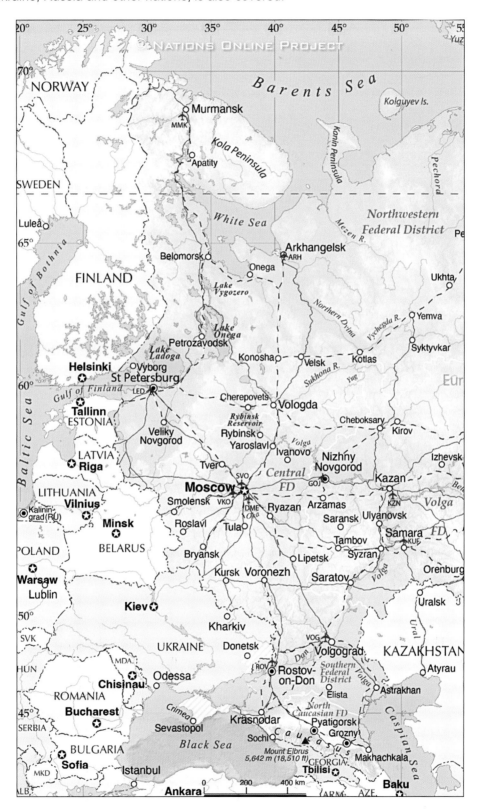

The timeline is the sixty years from 1962, the year of the Cuban missile crisis, up to the Russian invasion of Ukraine in 2022. The first thirty years of this period were the final years of the Soviet Union which had controlled the Soviet Republics as well as, after the Second World War, the three Baltic States plus aligned nations including Poland and East Germany.

Cuba

The new vessels **Metallurg Anosov** and **Poltava** were the best-known Soviet merchant ships to come to international attention in October 1962 when transporting missiles to Cuba as part of Operation Anadyr.

Operation Anadyr, named after a river in Far Eastern Russia, was the code name used by the Soviet Union for a daring plan to deploy in Cuba a number of ballistic missiles, medium-range bombers and a division of mechanised infantry to address the imbalance of strategic weapons and create an army group that could prevent an invasion of the island by United States forces. However, the operation was foiled when the United States discovered the plan, leading to what became known as the Cuban Missile Crisis. When its naval quarantine came into force on 24 October 1962, a total of 22 Soviet ships bound for Cuba were being watched by the United States, with **Poltava** one of the first to be intercepted.

The maritime effort to transport the Anadyr task force consisted of up to 200 trips, disguised as normal commercial voyages, by a total of 85 ships from nine ports in the summer of 1962. Ships' ultimate destinations were kept secret, even from their captains, as they sailed west under severe operational and communications restrictions. Cargo stowage on deck was minimised and, notwithstanding the hot conditions under deck, the 50,000 Soviet personnel transported in ships' holds were not allowed to emerge for fresh air until after dark.

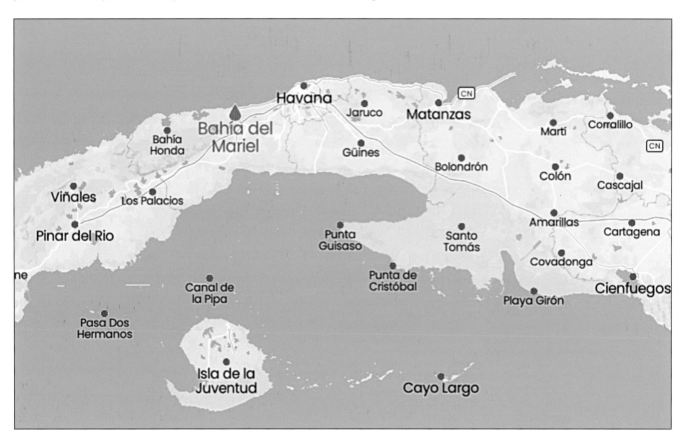

Following successful negotiations between the Presidents of the United States and Soviet Union in late October 1962, it was reported that the above mentioned two ships and seven others, named as **Bratsk**, **Divnogorsk**, **Ivan Polzunov**, **Labinsk**, **Volgoles**, **Fizik Kurchatov** and **Leninsky Komsomol**, had left Cuba by 10 November 1962 to return the offensive weapons to the Soviet Union.

Metallurg Anosov was one of 25 freighters of the project 567 type developed at the Central Design Bureau Chernomorsudoproekt in Nikolayev. Equipped with a steam turbine engine and capable of 19 knots, she was constructed by Kherson shipyard and completed on 29 September 1962. Operated by Black Sea Shipping Company of Odessa, it is understood that hold no.4 was temporarily converted for the transportation of 1,600 soldiers and that she had loaded at Nikolayev eight missiles and transporters, described as "special cargo", plus containers for rocket fuel stowed on deck, secretly bound for Bahia del Mariel (Mariel Bay) in Cuba (see map). Departing on 4 October, the vessel successfully navigated through a United States naval blockade but on 29 October the Soviet Union agreed to take the weapons out of Cuba. **Metallurg Anosov** returned to a Black Sea port on about 20 November and is thought to have been unloaded by 1 December 1962. Among the ships which subsequently served Cuba from the Baltic Sea were many of the East German fleet including the passenger/cargo ship **J.G.Fichte**, purchased by VEB Deutsche Seereederei in 1962.

Ukraine

Dnipro, on the Dniepr River in the centre of the map, is Ukraine's fourth-largest city. Four of the accompanying photographs were taken in the Dnipro area by Maksym Pysmennyi. The city was known as Dnipropetrovsk from 1926 until May 2016.

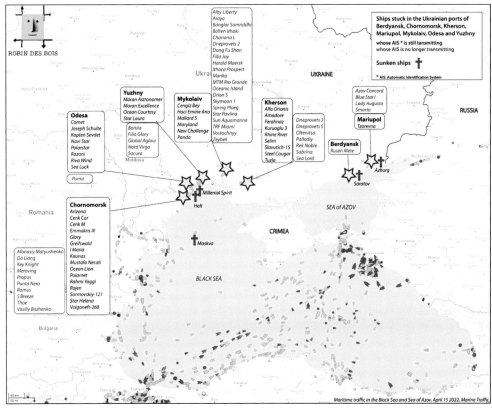

The map of the Black Sea and Sea of Azov, exclusively circulated in April 2022 by Association Robin des Bois, an organisation founded in France in 1985 by pioneers of environmental protection, shows the entrapment of a total of 93 merchant ships in March 2022 due to the Russian invasion of Ukraine which started on 24 February. It may be noted that about twenty of the ships were owned in Ukraine while half of the remainder were owned in either Greece or Turkey.

One of the trapped Ukrainian owned ships, the 2010 built bulk carrier *Arizona*, is commercially managed by Ocean Agencies Limited which was formerly the London base of Black Sea Shipping Company of Odessa. As at March 2023, this company operated ten geared bulk carriers built between 2003 and 2016 which are in part managed from Odessa by Staff Centre Ship Management or Unimor Shipping Agency, which manages a further six bulk carriers and four general cargo ships, and since April 2022 has an office in Varna.

Other major Ukrainian companies with trapped ships include Intresco, also of Odessa, which operates twelve ships including *Smarta* which remains trapped at Mariupol. The Kyiv based Ukrrichflot, which operates a total of twenty small ships, had four vessels trapped, the *Afanasiy Matyushenko* at Chernomorsk (since released) plus three of the *Dneprovets* type.

Notwithstanding the release from August 2022 of some ships laden with grain, including *Arizona* and *Sacura*, only ships berthed in the seaports of Odessa and Chornomorsk have been able to sail. The Southern Bug river including Mykolaiv port, located where it meets the Inhul River, remains closed to navigation, as does Kherson on the Dniepr river. As at 1 March 2023, renewed efforts are being made to extend the "Black Sea Grain Initiative" beyond the agreed expiration date of 18 March and also to release the ships trapped at Mykolaiv. Ships trapped for over twelve months will most probably be abandoned to insurance underwriters.

Meanwhile, the violence in Ukraine has sadly claimed many more lives including that of the businessman Oleksiy Vadaturskyi (1947-2022) and his wife Raisa at their home in Mykolaiv on 31 July 2022. Through his company NIBULON, the largest grain logistics company in Ukraine, he had greatly contributed to the Ukrainian economy, implementing a large-scale investment programme to revive Ukrainian rivers as transport arteries. In 2007 Vadaturskyi was awarded the "Hero of Ukraine", the country's highest honour, for his role in the development of Ukraine's agricultural industry. During 2020/21, his company exported 4.6 million tons of Ukrainian grain, established new trading relations with Bulgaria, shipped high-quality wheat to Saudi Arabia for the first time and started to ship rapeseed to the United Kingdom. Following the Russian invasion of Ukraine, and the grain export agreement reached with Russia on 22 July 2022, Vadaturskyi and his businesses were actively devising solutions to resume the normal flow of Ukrainian grain to countries in need.

Developments in merchant shipping of the Soviet Union, Ukraine, Russia, Georgia and the three Baltic States

1. Soviet Union

At the start of the Second World War the Soviet Union (U.S.S.R.), which was created by revolution in 1917, had an aged fleet of generally small ships. On 13 June 1922, the Council of Labor and Defence of the Republic established the state shipping companies Baltic, Northern, Black Sea-Azov and Caspian in the system of the People's Commissariat of Railways, and entrusted the general management of their activities to the Central Board of the State Trade Fleet. All freight movements were under the control of Sovfracht.

The joint-stock company Sovtorgflot was created in 1924 to manage the Soviet commercial fleet, directed from Moscow by the Ministry of the Maritime Fleet ("Minmorflot"). In January 1932 the People's Commissariat for Water Transport (Narkomvodtrans) divided the fleets of the regional main offices of Sovtorgflot between foreign and local trade, the latter being passed to the new Merchant Maritime Fleet of the Soviet Union ("Morflot"). Meanwhile, the Soviet state oil company Neftesindikat (Naptha Syndicate of the U.S.S.R.) entered the international market in 1922 to manage oil exports from the Black Sea to Mediterranean Sea ports, building its first ships in 1926, and in 1934 Sovtanker was created to manage the growing tanker fleet.

As the Soviet fleet was decimated during the Second World War, some ships were taken by way of reparation while others were gifted by the United Kingdom or loaned to the U.S.S.R. by the United States under the lend-lease arrangement. This was a concept introduced in 1941 by Franklin D. Roosevelt, the United States President from 1933 to 1945, to aid the Allies in their struggle against the Axis nations.

Admiral Sergei Gorshkov (1910-1988), who came to prominence following the 1962 Cuban missile crisis and subsequent fall of President Krushchev, had underlined that "a strong merchant fleet is an important element in the overall build-up of Soviet sea power." Although many new ships were built in Soviet yards, a large number were sourced by Sudoimport, the Soviet foreign trade organization with a monopoly on the foreign trade of ships, mainly from Finland, Poland, East Germany and Yugoslavia.

The Soviet Union's merchant fleet was thereby transformed into an important international trader with three functions: to earn hard currency on international trades, to support the Navy and to provide transportation of military and economic aid cargoes to and from other Communist nations. During the 1960s and 1970s these included

Bulgaria, Cuba, North Vietnam, the People's Republic of China and North Korea. For example, an Odessa to Vietnam cargo liner service commenced in 1961 and Odessa Ocean Line, linking Ilyichevsk and Saigon, was inaugurated in 1971. A joint service with Bulgaria, serving Bourgas from a range of Soviet Black Sea ports, started in 1963. In 1978 this was extended to a railway ferry service between Ilyichevsk and Varna.

During the 1970s the Soviet Union established several international cargo liner services including Baltic Shipping Company of Leningrad's Balt-Atlantic and Balt-Canada services to North America, Balt-Australia Line for which fifteen ships of the **Novgorod** type were built in Finland, Balt-Orient and Balt-Gulf. In May 1978, Balt-Atlantic was accepted into the Liner Conference which sought to control services between North Europe and the United States. Meanwhile, a Black Sea to Japan service was started in 1976. Other services out of Black Sea ports included Blasco Oriental Line from 1981, the year in which Odessa Ocean Line became a container service. Blasco Oriental Line employed large ro/ro ships, loading at Ilyichevsk and calling at Saigon, Da-Nang and Japanese ports, returning via Tartous in Syria and Mersin in Turkey.

A joint service with India, operating between ports in the Black Sea and Indian sub-continent commenced in 1956, followed in 1976 by the Indo-Soviet Shipping Service ("Sovindship") with Juzhflot of Moscow and The Shipping Corporation of India acting as managers. Opened in 1979 were Blasco Industan Line, calling at ports in north west Europe including Avonmouth and major ports in India, and the Gulfind service between Ilyichevsk, Mediterranean ports and Bombay. It was acknowledged that the U.S.S.R. merchant marine benefited from international co-operation, based on trust and equality of partners.

By 1980 the Soviet Union had an active seagoing merchant fleet of 7,495 ships and was said to be operating at market prices without ideological or political considerations, not undercutting world shipping costs. In the 1980 edition of his book "Soviet Merchant Ships", Ambrose Greenway noted that larger and more sophisticated ships were being built, with an increased emphasis on Ro-Ro and bulk fleets, including many vessels specifically designed for use in extreme northern latitudes, the location of much of the Soviet Union's mineral resources.

Container transportation developed in the Soviet Union in parallel to the rest of the world. As the volume of cargo transportation in containers increased, their transportation technology improved, as well as container handling technology in seaports, the design of container ships improved and their size increased. Specialised small-capacity container ships of the **Sestroretsk** and **Kapitan Sakharov** types were built at Vyborg and the **Alexander Fadeev** type at Kherson, but larger capacity ships, along with Lo-Ro ships of the **Astrakhan** type, were built at Warnemünde in East Germany. Ro-Ro ships of various types were built at Leningrad and Nikolayev, as well as at shipyards in Poland, Finland and France. For the transportation of goods in the Soviet Arctic, two series of specialised ro-ro ships of the Arctic class were built in Finland, the SA-15 project of the **Norilsk** type, with a container capacity of 532 TEU and the improved SA-15 super project, of the **Anatoly Kolesnichenko** type, with a capacity of 562 TEU. The fleet of container ships and other vessels then wholly met the nation's needs for container transportation around the world with Soviet container lines earning foreign currency while on charter to overseas companies.

From March 1973 Minmorflot was allowed to acquire new and second-hand vessels through bareboat charters, managed by Sovfracht, thereby using western financial institutions for Soviet fleet renovation. This innovative approach for the Soviet planned economy, leading to the creation of Sovcomflot in 1988, one of the first joint -stock commercial enterprises in the history of modern Russia, made it possible to renew the country's fleet and implement the most advanced technical, commercial and financial management systems. The first of over one hundred vessels purchased under the new scheme by 1988 were two bulk carriers, **Sovfrakht** (ex **Magdi**) and **Sovinflot** (ex **Olga**), operated until 1990 by Black Sea Shipping Company of Odessa.

The Soviet Union's Vietsovlighter ("VSL") joint venture with Vietnam was established in 1989 to operate three expensive barge carriers named **Indira Gandhi**, **Le Duan** and **Ernesto Che Guevara**. Managed by Yuriy Kanashevsky, the purpose of the joint venture was to solve the acute problem of idle lighters in Vietnamese ports, reduce commercial defects in the delivery of goods to recipients, increase the safety of lighters in ports, organize their repair at inexpensive Vietnamese ship repair bases and to generally reduce the costs of the operation.

Also, in June 1989, crews were ordered to join several ships which were transferred from Black Sea Shipping Company to the Maltese flag and registered under the nominal ownership of a series of companies given "Transblasco" names. Managed by the Piraeus based Transorient Overseas S.A., a joint venture with Transvek Holdings, the first of these ships were **Iason** (the former **Matesta**), **Olvia** (ex **Berezniki**), **Amfitriti** (ex **Millerovo**) and **Galini** (ex **Mozyr**).

By 1990, Sovcomflot had a capacity of 1.8m dwt, its ships since then largely operated under flags of convenience including Cyprus and Liberia. It was, for example, involved in the acquisition and management of three tankers named **Langepas**, **Urai** and **Kogalym** operated by Lukoil, an energy corporation formed in 1991, headed by Ravil

Maganov (1954-2022) and headquartered in Moscow, "Luk" representing the initials of those three oil-producing cities. In 1995, then under Russian state ownership, Sovcomflot was transformed into a joint-stock company. Sovcomflot was operating 134 vessels until its recent substantial divestment as a result of sanctions imposed following the invasion of Ukraine.

In 1990 the Soviet Union had the World's fifth largest fleet, with almost 25m dwt of shipping, but its break up in 1991 saw the fleet allocated between its constituent Republics and the regional shipping companies in Russia and Ukraine. All former Soviet Union ships were set to change to their new national flags by mid 1992 but many ships were sold to international buyers or scrapped.

The Commonwealth of Independent States (C.I.S.) was established on 21 December 1991 to coordinate the economies, foreign relations, defence, immigration policies, environmental protection and law enforcement on behalf of ten former Soviet republics. The Baltic states of Lithuania, Latvia and Estonia chose not to join the C.I.S. while Ukraine and Turkmenistan declined to ratify its creation agreement and Georgia withdrew in 2008 following an armed incursion by Russian forces. Ukraine remained an associate member of the C.I.S. until 2014, when it ceased to participate in most of its activities following the Russian annexation of Crimea; it withdrew completely in 2018 due to the conflict over the Donbass.

2. Ukraine

Black Sea Shipping Company

Black Sea Shipping Company was originally established at Odessa on 16 May 1833 as the Black Sea Society of Steamboats to establish communications between Odessa and Constantinople, but disappeared after the Crimean War of the 1850s.

In September 1922, soon after the Soviet Union was created, an office of the Black Sea and Azov Seas State Steamship Company was opened at Odessa and, from 18 July 1924, this became the local base of Sovtorgflot. In January 1927, an office was opened at the port of Mariupol, which between 1948 and 1989 was named Zhdanov after the Soviet functionary Andrei Zhdanov. In 1957 the Sovtanker fleet was integrated into Black Sea State Shipping Company which, on 16 February 1959, became Black Sea Shipping Company. In 1964, the tanker fleet was transferred into a separate division based at Novorossiysk and the Azov regional division became known as Black Sea Shipping Company's coal and ore division.

Following the dissolution of the U.S.S.R. in 1991, its Black Sea Shipping Company based fleet of almost 200 ships passed from the Ministry of Sea Fleet of the Soviet Union to the State Property Fund of Ukraine. Locally known as Chernomorskoye Morskoye Parokhodstvo ("ChMP"), from 3 August 1993 the company was internationally known as BLASCO. Several operating divisions were created including BLASCOBULK, managed by the experienced shipbroker Valeriy V.Markov, but the company suffered many ship arrests and sales at auctions before collapsing in 1996. Oddly, the funnel colours of BLASCO vessels were not uniformly painted. Most ships had a white funnel, most with black top, although some had a plain black funnel; the occasional ship had the Ukraine flag painted on the black funnel. More attractive were those painted with the Ukrainian trident, usually in a yellow circle on a blue band over a white funnel.

Many vessels, particularly general cargo ships, were old and obsolete, causing repair and other costs to significantly increase. Furthermore, the employment opportunities previously enjoyed when part of the Soviet Union were no longer available. Then, 93% of the cargoes carried were arranged by Sovfracht under Soviet foreign economic contracts, with 77% of cargo flows being from Russia, Belarus, the Baltic States and Asia, with only 7% of cargoes being arranged through CIF (Cost, insurance, and freight) contracts with foreign charterers. It is understood that BLASCO managers were still not allowed to engage in chartering, which was solely arranged by the Ministry of the Navy, but chartering offices were set up in London, Hamburg, Piraeus, Saigon, Singapore and New York.

The transfer of ships to the management of foreign companies or enterprises with mixed capital was therefore seen as a solution to the problem. The Black Sea Shipping Company therefore contributed further ships to the Soviet-Greek enterprise Transblasco and the Soviet-Vietnamese enterprise Vietsovlighter ("VSL"), operating the vessels under foreign flags, albeit as far as possible still with Ukrainian crews.

Thus, in 1991, two more general cargo ships built in 1967 were transferred to Transblasco companies. These ships were **Dubrovnik**, renamed **Daphne**, and **Aleksandr Blok**, renamed **Thallia**. In addition the 1971 built bulk carrier **Donuzlav** was transferred, to trade as **Daria**, and in 1993/4 Transblasco companies acquired the 1976/7 built bulk carriers **Irene** and **Gloria Deo**, which were sold in 1999. The passenger liner **Leonid Sobinov** was also transferred to a Transblasco company and managed by Transorient from 1990.

Also in 1991, ten general cargo ships built between 1964 and 1967 were transferred to VSL, joining the three new lighter carriers mentioned above, there being an opportunity to operate them between the ports of Southeast Asia. This step was taken both due to the age of the ships and the danger of their being arrested for debts in Europe or America. These ten ships were among the many sold for scrap between 1993 and 1996, with the barge carriers soon lying idle.

Efforts to save Black Sea Shipping Company

Seeking to minimise the scope for ship arrests, Pavel Kudyukin (born in Odessa in 1947), the managing director of BLASCO between 1992 and 1994, proposed to use the internationally adopted system of "one ship – one shipping company", so that a ship could only be detained for debts directly related to that ship, with BLASCO effectively becoming a holding company. Although this proposal was initially dismissed by the Government, in 1995, Kudyukin did achieve the creation of several subsidiaries, including Maddock Trading Company to nominally own the passenger ships *Gruziya*, *Kareliya* and *Kazakhstan*, but these initiatives did not save the company. In seeking to enforce payment by Black Sea Shipping Company of unpaid container rentals, legal action by Planmarine AG of Switzerland in 1997, involving the arrest in Nouméa of *Kareliya*, was temporarily thwarted. The ship was arrested on arrival at her next port of call, Haifa, and sold at auction.

In 1995, on being promoted to the position of technical manager of BLASCO's fleet of 43 bulk carriers, senior mechanic Vitaly Stepanovich Sergeychik noticed some financial inconsistencies in the system. A program for financial control of planning and expenditure was created and, following implementation of the necessary control measures, he was given the task of creating a well managed company that would demonstrate to foreign banks that ship management in Ukraine could be reliable. A subsidiary named UKMAR was thereby established in 1997 but, in order to achieve international success, it was necessary to establish UKMAR Ship Management in Limassol, Cyprus. However the "many nuances of joint ownership" slowed progress, causing Sergeychik to create Staff Center Ship Management in Odessa. This new company comprised ship management, crewing and repair departments which were successfully improved and expanded and were later separated into divisions of a group of companies.

Kudyukin who was, it seems unjustifiably, held responsible for the Company's financial collapse, believes that, given its past importance to Ukraine, the volume of grain exported and the historically large seafaring community in Odessa, the essence of Black Sea Shipping Company should be re-created in a new form and preliminary steps have been taken to that end.

Also controversial was the creation of joint ventures with foreign companies, for example that with V. Ships (Vlasov Group). Wishing to increase fleet efficiency with the help of experienced managers, Kudyukin had concluded a cooperation agreement with V. Ships to manage about fifty ships. V. Ships' Silver Line office in London was awarded the management of a series of similar vessels, some of which were given the names of England footballers. One example was the 1983 built *Shearer*, the former *Valentin Zolotaryev*, which was managed by V. Ships from 1996 until 2002, for the final four years as *Antwerp Bridge*. Subsequently renamed *Sea Dream*, managed by Strongtec and Sudoservice of Odessa and placed under the Georgian flag, she was sold in 2004. Other examples were *Valeriya Barsova*, as *Sheringham* from 1996, and the former *Aram Khachaturyan*, as *Hobson* from 1997, both of which were managed by Silver Line until 2000. The latter ship had briefly traded earlier in 1997 as *Azure America*, again managed by Strongtec.

Danube Shipping Company

The Soviet State Danube Shipping Company (SDGP), established at Izmail on 14 October 1944, which was considered to be primarily a sea going operation, was responsible for the mixed sea-river transportation of cargoes along the River Danube. SDGP was subordinated to Morflot and the word "State" was deleted from its name in 1959. In 1991, Soviet Danube Shipping Company was renamed Ukrainian Danube Shipping Company. As at March 2023, it is listed by Equasis as owning nine general cargo ships, six reefers and one tanker, but many of these ships may be idle.

Several barge carriers were operated by Soviet Danube Shipping Company. For the Soviet Union's Interlighter Line to India, the 1552 TEU capacity *Yulius Fuchik* (or *Julius Fucik*) and *Tibor Szamueli* were built in 1978 by the Valmet shipyard in Finland where the 855 TEU capacity *Boris Polevoy* and *Pavel Antokolsky* were built in 1984 for a service to the Red Sea. The 513 TEU capacity *Anatoliy Zheleznyakov* and *Nikolay Markin* were also built in 1984, by the Breda shipyard at Marghera, near Venice, to operate between Ust-Dunaysk, in the southern part of the Zhebriyans'ka Bay of the Black Sea, at the mouth of the Ochakiv estuary of the Danube delta, and eastern Mediterranean ports. Its barge carriers were all sold by 1998.

Fishing

Overseeing the Crimean fishing fleets on behalf of the Soviet Ministry of Fishing Industry were Sevastopol Administration of Ocean Fishing ("SUOR") and Kerch Administration of Ocean Fishing ("KUOR"). In 1962 the Ministry established Az-Cher-Ryba (Azov Black Seas fishing) to act as regional coordinator for the Azov and Black Sea Basin including Crimea. In January 1967 the "SUOR" operation was split between the Sevastopol division of trawling fleet ("SUTF"), known from September 1972 as the fishing production association "Atlantika", which then managed the sea fishing port, and Yugrybkholodflot to manage fish processing, transport and towing. Then, in December 1988, Yug-Ryba (South fishing) was created to oversee the growing fleet of trawlers, reefer ships, factory ships, rescue tugs and tankers. In the 1970s "KUOR" was replaced by "Kerchrybprom" but these Crimea based fleets stagnated in the 1990s. In addition the late Valeriy Kravchenko (1955-2002), who in 1993 took control of the struggling ARC "Antarktika", had sought without success to restore the fishing fleet of Ukraine. "Antarktika" was one of the largest fishing companies of the Soviet Union, operating out of Ilichevsk (now Chornomorsk) as far as West Africa.

Azov Shipping Company

History

Azov Shipping Company was founded on 1 December 1871 by the Jewish/Russian merchant Samuil Polyakov from Taganrog. His main objective was to develop maritime trade in the northern Black Sea region combined with rail connections from the Donetsk coal basin. The subsequent history of the company was inevitably linked with the port of Mariupol, its rapid development being suspended during the First World War and the civil war in the Russian Empire. Many of Azov's ships, as part of the red and white Azov naval fleets, were lost during the hostilities of 1920-1921. The pictured medal, celebrating 125 years of operation, was issued in 1996.

In 1931, when Morflot was created to manage the Soviet Union's short sea fleet, the Mariupol office became its regional headquarters. A further reorganisation in 1934 saw the creation of Tsumorflot within the People's Commissariat of Water Transport and the establishment of divisions based at Odessa and Mariupol, the latter known as the Azov division. In 1939 this was reconstituted by the newly created Peoples Commissariat of the Merchant Fleet of the U.S.S.R. as the Azov State Shipping Company. In 1941, for wartime reasons, Azov's base was located at Rostov-upon-Don.

Between July 1941 and December 1943 the Black Sea and Azov Seas divisions, together with Sovtanker, were temporarily merged into a Black Sea & Azov Basin division. Then, between September 1944 and March 1946, the ships involved were allocated to the two divisions which became known as Black Sea State Shipping Company and the Azov State Shipping Company. In 1953 the latter became the Azov regional division of Black Sea State Shipping company and its base was relocated back to Zhdanov.

With effect from 24 January 1967, the Azov and Novorossiysk fleets became independent from Black Sea Shipping Company and Azov Sea Shipping Company was created. Following the dissolution of the U.S.S.R., this latter company was renamed Azov Shipping Company and took ownership of the ships registered at the ports in its area. Most of the ships were registered at Zhdanov (later Mariupol) although some were based at Nikolayev (now Mykolaiv), Ilichevsk (now Chornomorsk), Izmail, Kherson and the Crimean ports of Sevastopol and Kerch.

Efforts to save Azov Shipping Company

In February 1989, Anatoliy Bandura (1946-2005) was appointed as managing director of Azov Shipping Company, which then operated more than one hundred ships, four ports on the Sea of Azov and three shipyards. He had worked for Azov Shipping since 1971, becoming a ship's captain and then deputy head of the company. On 18 March 1990, he was elected to the Verkhovna Rada (Parliament) of Ukraine, representing part of the Donetsk region, and subsequently sat on the Commission for economic reform and management of the national economy.

In 1991 Azov Shipping Company established a subsidiary company named Cometas Shipping, also based at Mariupol. The first of ten ships operated by Cometas was the 1965 built **Aleksandr Dovzhenko**, renamed **Dove**, while five of its ships had previously carried names commencing **Manley**, managed by Progressive Shipping of Athens in a joint venture with Azov Shipping. The prefix **Manley** derived from the involvement of the U.K. based Manley Hopkins & Co. (Manley Oceanwide Projects). The 1979 built **Manley Havant**, acquired in 1994, was in 1996 to be renamed **Mariupol Sun** but this failed to materialise and only in 2002 was she renamed **Donbass**. She was the last vessel to be operated by Cometas, latterly as **Sea Jay**, until 2010. Azov Shipping Company had also entered a joint venture with Sharaf Shipping Agency of Dubai. Named Gulf Azov Shipping ("GASCO"), between 1991 and 2002 it operated a total of six ships, all with names commencing **Dubai**.

However, the affairs of the Azov Shipping Company significantly deteriorated with several ships being arrested, not only for the debts of the Azov Shipping Company but also for the debts of Ukraine. During the 1990s, Azov Shipping Company decommissioned and sold almost two thirds of its ships, most being old and obsolete. At the end of 2000, Anatoliy Bandura was obliged to resign as head of the company.

Then, on 24 January 2003, the Donetsk Regional State Property Fund of Ukraine decided to transfer the remaining assets of Azov Shipping Company, including its residual fleet of 33 ships, to the newly created Commercial Fleet of Donbass (CFD Shipping Limited). This company was formed by the Donetsk based System Capital Management, headed by Rinat Akhmetov, who was born in 1966 at Donetsk and is owner and president of the football club Shakhtar Donetsk. He started business trading in coal and coke, subsequently buying the recently devastated Azovstal and Ilyich steel works at Mariupol. During the recent years of conflict, Akhmetov has provided much humanitarian assistance to the population of eastern Ukraine. However, debts incurred by Azov Shipping and the state of Ukraine resulted in the arrest of several CFD ships and it ceased trading in 2014, leaving **Vladimir Osiptsov** unaccounted for since March 2009 and **Vyacheslav Ilyin** laid up at the Azov Shipyard in Mariupol since December 2011. CFD's last trading vessel **Sky Star**, the former **VTC Star** purchased in 2011 from Vietnam Sea Transport & Chartering Co., was abandoned off Douala in West Africa.

Private Ukraine companies

Some successful private shipping enterprises have been created in Ukraine, albeit in the main as technical and crew managers, with many technically competent individuals working overseas. Their knowledge of seafaring, experience of communicating with foreign colleagues and good knowledge of the English language allowed such individuals to succeed in working with foreign partners. Over time, many hundreds of agency companies were opened in different cities of Ukraine - Odessa, Izmail, Mariupol, Kherson, Nikolaev, Kiev, Sevastopol, etc. - to arrange the employment of sailors on board ships of foreign owners.

Kaalbye Shipping is a notable Odessa based private company, created in 1996 by Capt. Igor Urbanski, then Deputy Minister of Transport and Communications, and the late Boris Kogan (1950-2017). Kaalbye International was subsequently created in the British Virgin Islands and its ships were registered under "flags of convenience". Capt. Urbanski, who was born in 1953 at Akhalkalaki, Georgia, graduated in 1976 from the Odessa Higher Marine Engineering School with a degree in navigation. Until 1994, he was a deck officer with the Black Sea Shipping Company. Kaalbye operated many general cargo ships between 1996 and 2018 and, under the name K & O Shipping, had an interest in passenger liners. Thus, the former Soviet liner **Gruziya** was operated from 1995 to 1998 as **Odessa Sky**, the former **Kareliya** from 1998 to 2004 as **Olvia** and the former **Shota Rustaveli** from 2000 to 2003 as **Assedo**.

During the early 1990s Aleksei Fedoricsev, a former professional footballer with Dynamo Moscow, who was born in 1955 at Krasnogorsk, Moscow Oblast, began trading in car parts and railway sleepers. He then became involved in logistics, concentrating on transporting and trading in grain, phosphates and sulphur. In 1996 he opened an office in Athens with Greek partners under the name Priamos Maritime S.A., until 2009 operating a number of bulk carriers, trading as FAM Bulkers. Fedoricsev had also invested in Ukraine, as Fedcom operating a fleet of bulk carriers from an office in Mariupol between 2003 and 2013, aided by Unimor Shipping Agency of Odessa and Ocean Agencies Limited of London. His Fedcominvest had also constructed some of Ukraine's largest grain terminals, but this success indirectly led to a legal dispute with the government which was not resolved until 2017.

3. Russia

A total of 11m dwt of ships, 56% of the Soviet fleet, was transferred to nine Russian companies supervised by a new maritime department within the Russian Federation's Ministry of Transport, based at the former Morflot premises in Moscow near the Kremlin. The nine Russian companies concerned were Baltic Shipping Company ("BSC"), Northern Shipping Company of Archangel ("NSC"), Murmansk Shipping Company, Novorossiysk Shipping Company, Far-Eastern Shipping Company ("FESCO") of Vladivostok, Arctic Shipping Company (North Eastern Department) of Tiksi and the Primorsk, Sakhalin and Kamchatka shipping companies. The development of the latter six companies falls outside the geographical scope of this book.

It was stated that a top priority would be given to the safety of Russian ships and the replacement of old and obsolete vessels. An immediate challenge however involved the re-financing of ten containerships costing USD 1bn which had been ordered from German yards to lease to Senator Linie and Deutsche Seereederei in a joint service with Cho Yang.

Baltic Shipping Company

BSC, originally founded in 1835 and resurrected in 1922 by the Directorate of Maritime Transport of the Baltic Sea (Baltmortran), became one of the largest of the Soviet Union's shipping companies. In November 1992 it was transformed into a joint stock company and attracted the attention of international investors including the U.K.'s Tufton Oceanic and Interorient of Cyprus but its financial problems led to many ship arrests and sales at auction in the mid-1990s followed by liquidation in 1996. Balt-Med Shipping Company, a joint venture with Gourdomichalis Maritime of Piraeus, was formed in 1992 to manage five of BSC's ships, including the former *Vereya* as *Ifigenia*, but this also closed in 1996. Altex Shipping of St. Petersburg, a company controlled by the Russian Government, was meanwhile founded in 1995 to trade six small Finnish built ships plus the 1978 built Ro/Ro *Ivan Derbenev* under the Russian flag, all previously operated by BSC.

In 1994 three containerships were transferred to the Cypriot flag and management of Uniship (Hellas), and subsequently to Delphic Shipping of Athens, to operate a transatlantic service named Morline. Thus, the 1978 built *Nadezhda Obukhova*, *Nikolay Golovanov* and *Khudozhnik Romas* traded as *Mor U.K.*, *Mor Canada* and *Mor Europe* until 1999. In addition, between 1995 and 1998, Euroshipping A/O of St. Petersburg took over at least nine vessels including *Olga Ulyanova* and *Valerian Kuybyshev*, the latter renamed *Euroshipping 6*, with the London based Pan Oceanic Ship Management involved in their commercial management.

Northern and Murmansk Shipping Companies

NSC, established at Archangelsk in 1922 as State Northern Shipping Company, became the main Northern office of Sovtorgflot in October 1924, from January 1931 reporting to Morflot. From August 1954, by then known as Northern State Shipping Company, it became subordinate to the Ministry of Maritime Fleet of the U.S.S.R. ("Minmorflot"). An August 1964 merger with Murmansk State Arctic Shipping Company lasted only until January 1967 and JSC Northern Shipping Company was created in December 1991.

The Murmansk state cargo and passengers shipping company was created on 22 September 1939. Then, on 15 March 1946, its name was changed to Murmansk State Shipping Company, also subordinate to Minmorflot, and on 25 June 1953 it absorbed Archangelsk Arctic Shipping Company to become Murmansk State Arctic Shipping Company. In 1967 it was renamed Murmansk Shipping Company and in January 1992 became JSC Murmansk Shipping Company.

Novorossiysk Shipping Company

Novorossiysk Shipping Company was created on 24 January 1967 from the tanker division of Black Sea Shipping Company. JS Novorossiysk Shipping Company (Novoship) was created on 10 November 1992, followed by JS Sovcomflot (SCF) – Novoship on 20 June 2007.

Many successful private shipping enterprises have also been created in the Russian Federation, for example ARRC Line (Atlantic Ro/Ro Carriers), created at Moscow in 1995. ARRC utilised former Soviet vessels, notably the large Astrakhan (Lo/Ro 18) class built between 1986 and 1992, supplemented by chartered in tonnage. JSC "Baltic Mercur" was created in St.Petersburg to act as general agent in Russia while Atlantic Ship Management was formed in Odessa to cover technical management and local crewing. Commercial offices were established at New York and Montréal and, following the creation in 2005 of CISN Group, services have been further expanded.

TK Nord Project LLC ("TKNP") of Arkhangelsk is another good example of a new shipping company established in the Russian Federation. As at March 2023, TKNP owns fifteen ships built between 1990 and 2006, its fleet comprising seven general cargo "**Gracht**" ships acquired from Spliethoff of Amsterdam between 2016 and 2021, four similar vessels, two new bulk carriers and two tankers. Other examples are Transmorflot LLC and MG-Flot LLC based at Akhty in Dagestan, east of Georgia, which as at March 2023 together operate 26 ships of varying types and Trans-Flot JSC based at Samara on the River Volga.

A significant development was the creation of joint ventures with foreign companies, for example with the Piraeus based Unimar Maritime Services which in 1992 was managing a total of twelve former Soviet vessels. By 1996 a total of twenty-two ships had been transferred from Northern Shipping Company, eight of which were given names commencing **Uni**, their funnel colours being similar to those of the Soviet Union but without the hammer and sickle.

Another Greek domiciled example was the Balthellas Group, established in 1991 to act as commercial manager and chartering arm for twelve general cargo single deck or 'tweendeck vessels owned by Soviet interests. Balthellas from 1996 managed seven vessels formerly owned by Baltic and Northern Shipping Companies which were all placed under the St.Vincent and Grenadines flag, again with Pan Oceanic Ship Management of London having an involvement. The last two of these ships, named **Veta** and **Tanya I**, were both sold in 2002.

4. Georgia

The Caucasus nation of Georgia, lying at the intersection of Eastern Europe and Western Asia with the ports of Batumi and Poti on the Black Sea, took control in 1992 of the ships operated by Georgian Shipping Company ("GESCO"), created by the Soviet Union in 1967. Its fleet had included the **Memed Abashidze**, the former **Dragon/Ionic Ferry** purchased in 1997, and the tankers **Kherson** and **Gelovani**. These ships were among those sold shortly before a new company, Ocean Shipping Company of Georgia ("Ocean"), was established at Tbilisi, the capital of Georgia, in 2000. In 2001 Ocean had a fleet of twelve product tankers, mainly former Soviet vessels and all built in the 1980s, technically managed by Columbia Shipmanagement of Limassol. The tankers **St.Mary** and **Queen T.** called at Stanlow on the Manchester Ship Canal in 2004 to load oil products.

Following the sale of the company in 2005 to the New York based Eastwind Maritime, all of the ships were renamed with a "**Wind**" suffix to trade as Georgian Tankers, commercially managed from London and technically managed from Singapore. As part of the transaction it was agreed that Georgian Tankers would manage the nation's maritime academy. However, expansion plans including the potential development of Georgia for international ship registry were halted by the political situation in 2008 and Georgian Tankers' ships were all sold or scrapped. The above mentioned two ships, respectively renamed **Aral Wind** and **Adriatic Wind**, were among many sold in mid 2009, the latter for scrap. Batumi State Maritime Academy continues to operate, using the small tanker **Cadet** as a training ship.

5. Baltic States

Latvia

On 29 October 1940, after Latvia was annexed by the U.S.S.R., all ships registered in the country were transferred to the Latvian state shipping company within the Soviet People's Commissariat of the merchant fleet. After being merged with the Baltic State Sea shipping company from 1941 to 1957, by then focused mainly on tankers, it was again merged with Baltic between June 1964 and January 1967 before becoming Latvian Shipping Company. From 13 September 1991 this became VAS Latvijas Kuģniecība - Latvian Shipping Company ("LSC") – which later became known as LSC SIA. In 2017 the Geneva based international energy and commodities group Vitol S.A. became the majority shareholder of the company. There are currently under the technical management of LSC SIA thirty-two modern tankers, built between 2006 and 2020 and mainly owned by Vitol, of which sixteen have names commencing **Elandra**: https://lscgroup.lv/en/fleet/

Estonia

In parallel, after Estonia was annexed by the U.S.S.R. on 29 October 1940, all ships registered in that country were transferred to the Estonian state shipping company within the Soviet People's Commissariat of the merchant fleet. Between 1953 and 1956 this activity was downgraded to a subsidiary of Baltic state shipping company, known as Tallinn regional division of merchant fleet. Then reverting to Estonian state shipping company, on 24 January 1967 it became Estonian Shipping Company ("ESCO"). In December 1991 this became Eesti Merelaevandus AS, operating as Eesti Merelaevandus Estonia Line (E.M.E.L.). At its peak operating over ninety vessels, during the 1990s ESCO was in steady decline and, in 2001, was acquired by the Norwegian owned Tschudi Shipping Company. Then becoming Tschudi Ship Management A/S, ESCO's technical department currently offers a variety of services connected with diverse activities including offshore wind turbine support: https://www.tschudishipmanagement.com/about-tschudi

Lithuania

In May 1965, in order to improve the operations of tankers based at Klaipeda in Lithuania, a regional Klaipeda maritime agency of the Baltic sea shipping company was created. Then, effective from 1 January 1969, Klaipeda maritime agency was transformed into Lithuanian Shipping Company, its first vessels being the Liberty ships *Ivan Polzunov*, *Kuban*, *Pskov* and *Sevastopol*. In December 1991 it became the Lithuanian owned company JS Lietuvos Juru Laivininkyste ("LISCO").

After operating a total of over seventy vessels LISCO sold its last four ships in 2016. Its funnel colours were for some reason changed in the early 2000s. Examples of ships with the old and new Lithuanian funnel colours are included in the illustrations.

Conclusion

It has clearly been difficult for former Soviet Republics to adapt to the international containerised market conditions in which the global liner shipping industry now operates. Other than in the Russian Far East, they have lost their container transport independence and are completely dependent on foreign ship owners. Russia is however largely self sufficient in both dry and liquid bulk transport and in the shipping of liquefied natural gas. In addition, Russian shipping managers have been more successful in maintaining a presence in ship owning than their counterparts in Ukraine, the Baltic States and Georgia.

In Russia, the traditional importance of the nation's river network has long supported academies of water transport at Nizhniy Novgorod on the River Volga and at Rostov-on-Don, St.Petersburg, Novosibirsk and Moscow. Maritime academies also existed at Murmansk, Novorossiysk and Sevastopol. In 1944, the Soviet State Defence Council established the Leningrad Higher Marine Engineering College, from 1949 known as The Admiral Makarov High School of Marine Engineers; in December 1990 it was awarded the status of Academy. Then, in 2012, it was merged with the St.Petersburg State University for Waterway Communications to become The Admiral Makarov State University of Maritime and Inland Shipping ("SUMIS").

Ukrainian seafarers have traditionally received a high level of professional maritime education and experience and are willing and able to enter the international labour market in competition with seafarers from other countries such as Croatia, Poland, India and the Philippines. In 2002, in order to supplement the long established maritime academies in Odessa and Kiev, where future sailors and captains are trained, a new naval academy was opened in Kherson. Sub-faculties of Odessa National Maritime Academy were also opened at Izmail and Mariupol with certification and medical centres opened in Odessa, Izmail, Kherson, Chornomorsk and Mariupol.

Information Sources

The development of the Soviet Union's merchant shipping from the Bolshevik Revolution in 1917 until 1950 was described in detail by Martin J.Bollinger in his book "From the Revolution to the Cold War", published in 2012 by the World Ship Society. In 1969 Ambrose Greenway reacted to the post-war expansion of the Soviet merchant ship fleet by producing a book listing the vessels then in service, followed between 1976 and 1980 by revised editions slanted more towards ship recognition. Miramarshipindex.nz, Equasis.org and Fleetphoto.ru websites have been among other sources of information consulted during the research for this book.

Contents

Cuba Callers in the 1960s...........13
Ukraine Callers in the 2020s.......18
Historic Soviet Union Ships........20
Soviet Liners...............................26
Soviet Ships in the Bosphorus
Azov Shipping Company...............28
Black Sea Shipping Company.......30
Soviet Danube Shipping Co...........31
Novorossiysk Shipping Co.............32
Soviet Union Ships
Leninskiy Komsomol Type.............33
Ice Strengthened..........................34
Rostock Built.................................35
Warnemünde Built.........................36
Hungarian Built.............................37

Polish Built....................................38
Finnish Built..................................40
Soviet Built....................................42
Tankers...44
Soviet Firsts..................................45
Ukraine Ships
Black Sea Shipping Company.......46
Azov Shipping Company...............49
Gulf Azov Shipping Company........50
Cometas & Ukrainian Danube.......51
Crimea Based...............................52
Other Ukrainian Companies..........54
Kaalbye Shipping..........................56
Fedcom..59
Joint Ventures..............................60

Russian Ships
Northern Shipping Company.........61
Murmansk Shipping Company.......64
White Sea & Onega Shipping Co. .65
Baltic Shipping Company...............66
Novorossiysk Shipping Co.............68
Other Companies..........................69
Joint Ventures..............................75
Suez Visitors in the 1990s..........77
Georgian Ships...........................80
Baltic States
Estonia...81
Latvia...82
Lithuania......................................84

Metallurg Anosov in the St.Lawrence River passing Verchères, Québec, in icy conditions on 20 December 1980 bound for Odessa. She served the Soviet Union until early 1986 when sold through intermediaries to Chinese breakers. After departing from Ilichevsk in January 1986 for Cienfuegos in Cuba, she loaded a final cargo for Vladivostok and was sold, to be renamed *Anosov* and placed under the Cayman Islands flag. Soon resold to Chinese breakers, she arrived at Qinhuangdao on 22 May 1986 for scrapping. (*Marc Piché*)

Leninskiy Komsomol, the lead ship of the 19 knot project 567 type, departing from Montréal on 5 August 1983 bound for Cuba with a cargo of grain. Delivered at Kherson into the management of Black Sea Shipping Company on 23 December 1959, she had made two voyages from the U.S.S.R. to Cuba between September and November 1962, departing from Casilda, near Cienfuegos, on 10 November. She subsequently served the Soviet Union until February 1986 when sold for scrap and renamed *Ungur* at Odessa before departing for the breakers. (*Marc Piché*).

The Archangel registered **Poltava** off Gibraltar in 1969. Built at Nikolayev in 1962, she was initially registered at Odessa, transferred to Archangel in 1968 and into the fleet of Azov Shipping Company in 1976. Following a final voyage from Nikolayev to Kandla in April 1989, she proceeded to the beaches at Alang for breaking. (*Michael Lennon*)

Ivan Polzunov, berthed alongside Gibraltar's north mole during 1969, was an EC2-S-C1 type Liberty ship built at Richmond, California in 1943 as **Charles E. Dureya**, named after the pioneering American motor engineer. She was immediately passed to the Soviet Union under lend-lease arrangements to serve during wartime as the Vladivostok registered **Orel**. On being transferred to Black Sea Shipping Company in 1949 she was renamed **Ivan Polzunov**, so named in honour of the engineer who had created the first steam engine in Russia. One of four Liberty ships transferred to the newly formed Lithuania Shipping Company at the end of 1968, following a further voyage to Havana in March 1972, she finally arrived at Klaipeda in February 1973 and is thought to have been scrapped locally. (*Michael Lennon*)

The Kherson built project 567 type **Fizik Kurchatov** at Gibraltar on 14 August 1966. She was brand new when sailing to Cuba in October 1962. Delivered into the management of Black Sea Shipping Company on 30 June 1962, she served the Soviet Union until early 1986 when sold, to be renamed **Kurchat** and placed under the Cayman Islands flag. After departing from Ilichevsk in February 1986 for Havana, she loaded a final cargo for the North Korean port of Nampo. Soon resold to Taiwan breakers, she arrived at Kaohsiung on 24 July 1986 for scrapping. (*Michael Lennon*)

Bratsk, one of the Equator class built in 1957 at Turku in Finland, passing Portishead inbound for Avonmouth on 31 August 1967 during a voyage from Hamilton, Ontario. It is believed that, following a final voyage from Delfzijl to her home port of Leningrad in April 1982, *Bratsk* was broken up locally. (*Author*)

The Odessa registered *Labinsk*, a Polish B54 type built at Gdansk in 1960 and operated by Black Sea Shipping Company, sailing from Liverpool on 16 December 1979 following discharge of a cargo of Indian rice bran and cottonseed. Following a voyage from Da-Nang in Vietnam to Ilichevsk in November 1986 she again sailed to India, from there proceeding in February 1987 to Gadani Beach in Pakistan for scrapping. (*Author*)

Divnogorsk, a Polish B54 type built at Szczecin in 1961 and operated by Black Sea Shipping Company, in Singapore Roads on 16 March 1984. It is reported that, following a final voyage from Yuzhnyy to China during February 1986, *Divnogorsk* was scrapped at Huangpu. (*Ian Shiffman*)

Volgoles, photographed at Aberdeen in April 1975, was a B514 type built at Gdansk in 1960. Allocated to the Baltic Shipping Company of Leningrad, she served the Soviet Union until sold in 1989 to Zulacar Maritime of Piraeus and renamed *Milos J*. Following a voyage to Matadi at the end of 1989 she soon proceeded to the beaches at Alang in north western India for breaking. (*Alastair Paterson*)

J.G.Fichte berthed at Havana in September 1963. Purchased in August 1962 by VEB Deutsche Seereederei of Rostock, East Germany, specifically to provide a cargo, training and passenger service to Cuba, she had been built at Saint-Nazaire in 1950 as *Claude Bernard* for Compagnie Maritime des Chargeurs Réunis. Sold in mid 1979, she was renamed *Sunrise IV* for an intended single voyage to Taiwan for breaking but arrived at Karachi on 21 September 1979 and from there made her way to Colombo, arriving on 3 January 1980. Following a long period of lay up at Colombo she arrived at Gadani Beach on 24 May 1981 as *Pegancia* for breaking. (*Capt. Norbert Schmidt*)

In early 1962 East Germany began to build at Warnemünde a new series of ships, known as the X type, for trading to Cuba and elsewhere, the first being *Edgar Andre*, delivered on 31 October 1962. Deutsche Seereederei's XA type *Käthe Niederkirchner*, photographed at anchor off Southend in June 1965, famously stranded in Pentland Firth off the north coast of Scotland near the island of Muckle Skerry on 23 August 1965 during a voyage from Matanzas in Cuba to Rostock with a cargo of 9000 tonnes of sugar. It is understood that, seeking to save time, the Politoffizier had ordered the vessel's master to pass through Pentland Firth. Fortunately all on board were safely landed at the lighthouse. (*Alex Duncan*)

Dneprovets-2 was photographed on 30 May 2019 at Dnipro on the River Dnepr, south east of Kiev. Currently no ships are able to call at the port until safe access from the Black Sea via Kherson is restored. *Dneprovets-2* was built in 1988 at Rybinsk, at the confluence of the Volga and Sheksna Rivers, in Russia. Operated by Ukrrichflot JSC of Kiev, she is now trapped at Mykolayiv (Nikolayev). Of the nine ships with *Dneprovets* names built between 1987 and 1992, six remain with Ukraine while Russia operates *Dneprovets-8* as *Kudma 3*, Iran owns *Dneprovets-7* as *Kasra 1* and Bulgaria operates *Dneprovets-1* as *Briz*, which in 2004 was converted for use as an LPG tanker. (*Maksym Pysmennyi*)

The 1972 Komarno, Czechoslovakia, built *Mila*, the former *Volgo-Balt 164*, sailing from Port-Saint-Louis-du-Rhône, France, on 25 January 2003. Owned since 1994 by Excelsior Shipping & Trading, she was then operated by North-Western Shipping Company of Taganrog, Russia. Since 2004 *Mila* has been managed by Argo Shipping Company of Kherson, Ukraine, and until 2017 was registered in Cambodia. She was then moved to the Tanzanian flag but switched to Moldova in July 2020 and, following an Italian state control ban due to a failure to carry out essential repairs, moved to the Togo flag in June 2022. *Mila* sailed from Chioggia in Italy on 10 May 2022, and subsequently from Turkey in July, in each case bound for the south western Ukraine port of Izmail in the Danube Delta where port congestion is severe. (*Author*)

Oltenitsa departing from Sevastopol on 30 July 2012. A project M1565 sea/river type ship built in 1988 at Oltenita in Romania, she is owned by Don-2 Shipping Ltd and managed by Ukrrichflot Joint Stock Shipping Company of Kiev. Between 1968 and 1990, Şantierul Naval Olteniţa constructed 106 sea/river ships of the *Volgo-Don* type, commencing with *Volgo-Don 5000*, for the Soviet Union. Of these, only the 1986 built *Volgo-Don 5091* and *5095* were also of the M1565 type, the former now being operated by Russia. Since 2004, *Volgo-Don 5095* has been owned by Don-1 Shipping Ltd and managed by Ukrrichflot as *Oleksiy Federov*, as which she has been lying at Kherson since September 2021. Following a voyage from Saraylar in Turkey, *Oltenitsa* arrived at Kherson on 4 February 2022 and is now trapped. (*Volodymyr Knyaz*)

The 2010 Zhoushan built, Dolphin 57 type, Liberia flagged bulk carrier **Arizona**, commercially managed by Ocean Agencies Limited (formerly Blasco U.K.), was trapped at Chornomorsk from 19 February 2022 until released on 8 August 2022 to sail for Iskenderun with a cargo of grain. She subsequently proceeded to the Egyptian port El Dekheila, near Alexandria, to load for Searsport in Maine, United States. Ocean Agencies Limited currently manages ten bulk carriers built between 2003 and 2016 plus the 2009 built general cargo ship **Janis**, built as **Beluga Facility** and acquired in February 2023. **Arizona** was photographed near Escobar in the Paraná de Las Palmas River, Argentina, on 12 May 2021 (*Maxi Alonso*)

Slavutich-15, which was built at Kiev in 1990 for the Soviet Union, berthed at the 391 km point of the Dnepr river on 16 December 2018. Passing to Intersectoral State Association Ukrrichflot in 1992, she carried the name **Nattem VIII** between 1993 and 1996, when sailing under the flag of Malta, followed between 2001 and 2007 as **Sunrise III** under the flags of Georgia, Belize and the Comoros Islands. Since 2011, **Slavutich-15** has been managed by Delta Shipping Agency of Mariupol but is now trapped at Kherson, as are her Ukrrichflot operated sisterships **Slavutich-16** and **Slavutich-17**. A total of 18 **Slavutich** D-080M sea/river type ships were built by Kiev shipyard between 1981 and 1992. Of these, three have been scrapped while the remainder are operating under various flags. (*Maksym Pysmennyi*)

Vasiliy Bozhenko, a Sormovskiy 1557 type, was built in 1984 by the Krasnoye Sormovo Shipyard at Gorkiy for the Soviet Union's Main Directorate of the River Fleet under the Council of Ministers of the Ukrainian Soviet Socialist Republic. From 1992, she has been operated by the Intersectoral State Association Ukrrichflot and is seen in the upper roadstead of Dnipro river port on 4 October 2021. Following a voyage from Samsun in Turkey, she arrived at Chornomorsk on 17 February 2022 and was trapped there until August 2023. (*Maksym Pysmennyi*)

Msta, built at Helsinki in 1945 and taken over by the Soviet Union before completion, sailing from Avonmouth on 31 March 1965 bound for Rostock. The second of thirty-one timber carriers of the Khasan type built between 1945 and 1955, she was registered at Leningrad until 1955, then until 1969 at Murmansk, where she was partially rebuilt and modernised, and was finally based at Riga in Latvia. Her last reported movement was from Antwerp on 2 February 1971 bound for Riga. It seems that she was then renamed *Zutis*, hulked in Latvia from 1975 and broken up in November 1990. (*Author*)

Otto Shmidt photographed at Gibraltar in 1970. There is room for doubt about her identity. The 1914 built ship of that name, which was delivered to Van Nievelt, Goudriaan as *Bellatrix* and passed to the Soviet Union in 1934, when briefly named *Pskov*, was reported as having been deleted from the Soviet register in 1951 and later broken up. The same Dutch owner's 1915 built *Procyon* was sold to the Soviet Union in December 1934 for operation from Leningrad, initially as *Novgorod* but from 1935 as *Magnitogorsk*. Interned in Germany on 22 June 1941 and renamed *Trostburg*, she sank on 21 November 1944 during an air attack in Hamburg. It is understood that she was towed to Leningrad in July 1950 and rebuilt, emerging as this *Otto Shmidt*. Her last recorded voyage was from Szczecin on 30 April 1974 bound for Leningrad. (*Michael Lennon*)

The 1920 built **Mendeleev** served the Soviet Union from 1945 to 1970. Delivered at Harriman in the northern section of Bristol, Pennsylvania, to the United States Shipping Board as **Yapalaga**, she was operated by Waterman S.S. as **Beauregard** from 1940 until transferred to the Soviet Union on a lend-lease basis. Initially registered at Vladivostok, she was transferred to the Baltic Shipping Company in 1964. Photographed passing Maassluis West, outbound from Rotterdam, probably in early September 1966, her last voyage away from the U.S.S.R. commenced on 27 March 1969 from Alexandria to Klaipeda, calling at Gibraltar on 5 April. She was broken up in the U.S.S.R. during 1970. (*Koos Riedijk*)

Akademik Krylov, operated between 1946 and 1975 by the Baltic Shipping Company, was built at Flensburg in 1937 as **Mathias Stinnes**. Taken as a prize by British forces at Copenhagen in May 1945, she was briefly named **Empire Teviot** before being allocated to the Soviet Union. Photographed outbound from Rotterdam, her final voyage was from Halifax, Nova Scotia, to Leningrad in December 1975. (*Hans Krayenbosch*)

Vtoraya Pyatiletka was a First World War standard build ship, launched as **West Hasson** on 16 September 1919 at Portland, Oregon, by the Columbia River Shipbuilding Corporation for the United States Shipping Board. Delivered in October 1919 as **Siletz**, she was laid up at Norfolk, Va. for several years. In 1937 the functions and fleet of the Shipping Board were transferred to the newly created Maritime Commission and in March 1942 **Siletz** was passed into the operational management of Grace Line. However, in December 1942 she was taken over by the Soviet Union through lend-lease arrangements and registered at Vladivostok, managed by the Far Eastern Shipping Company. Renamed **Vtoraya Pyatiletka**, in 1946 she was transferred to the Black Sea Shipping Company of Odessa. Believed photographed at Alexandria shortly before sailing for the Black Sea on 6 January 1967, she was soon sold to breakers at La Spezia where she arrived on 10 June 1967. (*Author's Collection*)

Ilichevsk, photographed off Gibraltar on 9 May 1964, was built by Furness Shipbuilding at Haverton Hill, Teesside, in 1924 as *Tramore* for Johnston Line. In 1925 she passed to Prince Line and was renamed *Brazilian Prince* but in 1933 was sold to the Soviet Union to trade as *Voroshilov*, managed by Black Sea Shipping Company. Having been struck by an aerial torpedo when off Tuapse on 20 March 1942 and bombed at Novorossiysk on 2 July 1942, she was raised after 1945, rebuilt and re-engined in 1950. Probably for the reason that the Stalinist military officer Klim Voroshilov in whose honour she was named had fallen out of favour with the Kremlin, she was renamed *Ilichevsk* in 1962. Last reported passing Istanbul southbound in June 1972, it is thought that she was scrapped in 1975. (*Michael Lennon*)

The ice breaker *Sibiryakov* was photographed at Gibraltar in 1970. Built at Rotterdam in 1926 as *Jääkarhu* for the Finnish Government, she was handed over to the Soviet Union as war reparation in February 1945 and based at Leningrad. She was named in honour of Alexander Sibiryakov, a Russian Arctic explorer. Rebuilt in the 1950s, *Sibiryakov* served the Soviet Union until sent to La Spezia in 1972 for breaking. (*Michael Lennon*)

The 1960 Turku, Finland, built **Almetjevsk** was photographed in Kiel Bay from a passing Jahre Line ferry on 19 January 1975 when bound from Ventspils to Hamburg to load for the Caribbean. An example of the twelve "Dolinsk" type of the Equator class which were constructed by Wärtsilä Crichton-Vulcan at Turku between 1959 and 1961, she was operated by Baltic Shipping Company until sailing from Singapore Roads on 14 July 1986 bound for Russia, where it is assumed that she was soon scrapped. (*Author*)

The 1956 Bordeaux built **Ivan Sechenov**, one of the Black Sea Shipping Company managed fleet, was photographed at anchor off Istanbul on 14 September 1976, having recently arrived from the Black Sea. On 12 January 1977, when westbound from Istanbul, the vessel sank with the very sad loss of twenty-two of her crew following a collision with the ore carrier **Nicolas Maris** in dense fog off Canakkale. (*Author*)

The Soviet Danube Shipping Company's 1967 Budapest built **Kalmius**, photographed in the Bosphorus from a passing ferry on 22 December 1975, was one of a large number of similar ships built for the Soviet Union. She passed to the Ukrainian Danube Shipping Company in 1991 and continued trading until arriving at Setubal on 4 November 1999. There, seeking to recover unpaid wages, the crew took strike action. She was registered in Cambodia during 2000, sailing for Lisbon on 7 May 2001 and probably soon thereafter scrapped locally. (*Author*)

Janis Rainis (or *Yanis Raynis*) at Gibraltar in March 1964. Built in Belgium in 1908 as *St.Johann* for Rob. M. Sloman of Hamburg, as *Wotan* she had been taken over in 1919 by the Shipping Controller of London. Arundale S.S. Company operated the ship as *Berkdale* from 1926 until her sale in 1933 to Mrs F. Grauds of Riga, Latvia, to become *Everolanda*. Seized by the Soviet Union in June 1940, on 7 July 1941 she struck a mine in Kunda Bay, Estonia, was towed to Leningrad and beached. Refloated in November 1942, she was repaired and resumed trading in 1945 as *Janis Rainis*. Returned to Latvia in 1955, she was last reported sailing from Liverpool for Riga on 18 October 1968. Breaking commenced at Tallinn on 14 August 1969. (*Bert Warwick*)

Akademik Pavlov, also photographed at Gibraltar, was a lend/lease acquisition by the Soviet Union in 1945 from the United States. She was built at Kearny, New Jersey, in 1919 as *The Lambs*, was renamed *Exporter* in 1927 and then *Winona* in 1937, owned by Weyerhaeuser S.S. Co. Inc. of Tacoma. Modernised in the 1950s, her final voyage was from Antwerp in September 1973 to Leningrad. (*Michael Lennon*)

Kuban off Gibraltar in 1970, it is thought decked out with flags to celebrate the safe landing of the manned *Soyuz 9* spacecraft on its return to Earth on 19 June. She had called at Gibraltar during a voyage from Leningrad to Arbatax on the western coast of the island of Sardinia. *Kuban* was an EC2-S-C1 type Liberty ship launched at Portland, Oregon in 1943 as *William G.T'Vault*. The vessel was delivered to the Soviet Union under lend-lease arrangements to serve in wartime under Vladivostok registry. *Kuban* was passed to Leningrad registry in 1949 and late in 1968 to Klaipeda in Lithuania where she was hulked in January 1972 and used as a floating warehouse from May 1974 until scrapped in 1979. (*Michael Lennon*)

Zapadnaja Dvina, built by Wärtsilä Crichton-Vulcan at Turku, Finland, in 1955. She was departing from the Kiel Canal's Brunsbüttel Locks on 8 March 1975 during a voyage from Klaipeda to Antwerp. One of the final ships of a forty strong series which commenced in 1945 with the *Khasan* (see Msta on page 20) and concluded in 1956 with *Dnestr* and *Donets*, she was allocated by the Soviet Union to Northern Shipping Company of Archangel. The last reported movement of *Zapadnaja Dvina* was sailing from Gdynia on 4 May 1979 bound for Murmansk where it is thought she was broken up in 1982. (*Author*)

The Leningrad based Academy of Science's space research vessel *Nevel*, built in 1966, departing from Brunsbüttel Locks westbound on 21 June 1969. *Nevel* was one of four Project 596 type ships built by the A.Zhdanov yard at Leningrad between 1963 and 1968 which were completed as research vessels; the others were *Borovichi*, *Kegostrov* (built as *Taymyr*) and *Morzhovets*. Another four of the type, including the lead ship of the series, *Vytegrales*, were converted between 1974 and 1978 to serve as a fleet of space control and monitoring ships known as the "Star Flotilla"; the others were the former *Yeniseiles* (or *Eniseyles*), *Nazar Gubin* and *Semyon Kosinov*. Until 1994, the main tasks of the vessels were the reception and analysis of telemetry data and the provision of radio communications between spacecraft and the Mission Control Centre. While three of the ships were withdrawn from service by 2001 and presumed scrapped, *Kosmonaut Viktor Patsaev* (the former *Semen Kosinov*) was thereafter moored at the Kaliningrad Historical Museum of the World Ocean, until September 2017 providing communication with the International Space Station. In January 1990 *Nevel* was sent to Alang for breaking, soon to be followed there by her three sister research vessels. (*Author*)

Aleksandr Suvorov, named after a renowned Russian military commander, was an EC2-S-C1 type Liberty ship built at Portland, Oregon in 1943 as *Elijah P. Lovejoy*, named after the American Presbyterian minister and newspaper editor. The brand new vessel was immediately passed to the Soviet Union under lease-lend arrangements to serve in wartime under Vladivostok registry. Passed to Murmansk in 1946 and to Azov Shipping in 1968, she is seen on one of her final voyages, southbound in the Bosphorus on 4 September 1977. (*Author*)

The much-loved liner **Aleksandr Pushkin**, built at Wismar in 1965 for operation by Baltic Shipping Company, arriving at Turku on 3 July 1982. Moving in 1985 to the Far East, she was operated by CTC Cruises until leaving Hong Kong on 2 October 1989 for Vladivostok. Sent to Singapore in February 1990 for repairs, she emerged in May 1991 as **Marco Polo** for a voyage to Greece for renovation. Returned to service early in 1993, she operated successfully in European waters for ten years from 2010 with Cruise & Maritime Voyages until laid up and sent to Alang for scrapping. (*Krzysztof Brzoza*)

Adzhariya, the last of 19 Mikhail Kalinin-class passenger ships built for the Soviet Union between 1958 and 1964 by VEB Mathias Thesen Werft at Wismar in East Germany, northbound in the Bosphorus on 25 May 1981. She continued to be employed cruising out of Odessa until 1989 but was sent to Aliaga for breaking in January 1996. (*Dave Salisbury*)

Ukraina, built at Copenhagen in 1938 as *Basarabia* for Romania to serve, together with sister *Transilvania*, between Constantza and Alexandria, off Istanbul in September 1976. While both ships were laid up at Istanbul for most of the 1940s, only *Transilvania* returned to service when the war ended. *Basarabia* was ceded to the U.S.S.R. on 8 January 1945 as war reparation and renamed *Ukraina*. She then briefly served the Soviet navy as a submarine base before resuming employment as a passenger liner in 1946, mainly operating in the Black Sea and Mediterranean. Following a final return voyage from Havana to Odessa in August 1986, she sailed as *Ina* to Alang for scrapping. (*Author*)

The 1963 Wismar built *Nadezhda Krupskaya* which, other than participating in the 17th Soviet Antarctic Expedition during 1971/73, had normally been employed cruising out of Leningrad, was renamed *Kuban* late in 1975 and transferred to the Soviet Navy. In 1992 *Kuban*, photographed northbound in the Bosphorus in mid September 1976, became an ambulance transport for the Red Banner Black Sea Fleet based at Sevastopol. It was reported that, in July 1994, *Kuban* was sold to Bulgaria and renamed *Susana* for use as a floating casino. She was sent to Aliaga in February 1998 for breaking. (*Author*)

The Odessa based *Litva*, seen at speed off Istanbul in mid September 1976 while heading towards the Bosphorus and Black Sea, was built at Wismar in 1960. She was renamed *Boguchar* in 1988 for services between Ukraine and Istanbul but in 1992 a planned renaming as *Odessa Dream* was abandoned. She was sold in 1993 to Chinese buyers and renamed *Fu Jian* to provide passenger services between Hong Kong, Fuzhou and Xiamen. Planned to be sold for scrap in 2000, she instead proceeded to Luanda as *Green Coast* for use as an accommodation ship but unfortunately capsized there on 4 November 2006. (*Author*)

SOVIET SHIPS IN THE BOSPHORUS
AZOV SHIPPING COMPANY

The 1956 Gdansk built B31 type **Adam Mitskevich** northbound in the Bosphorus on 23 May 1981. Initially registered at Murmansk, she was transferred to Zhdanov registry in 1974 for operation by Azov Shipping Company. Last reported sailing from Zhdanov early in June 1985, she arrived at Valencia on 28 June 1985 for breaking. (*Dave Salisbury*)

Smela, built at Rostock in 1954 as one of the 19 strong Kolomna type 201, working cargo off Istanbul in July 1983 while operating out of her home port of Zhdanov. With two coal fired boilers and a double compound main steam engine, she was one of the last steamers built by Neptun Werft. She was allocated to Black Sea Shipping Company until 1969 and then transferred to Azov Shipping Company. It is understood that she was used as a training ship from the mid 1980s until beached at Aliaga on 23 July 2006 for scrapping. (*David Oldham*)

The 1957 Stocznia Gdanska built B31 type **Severomorsk** northbound on 22 April 1981. A large number of B31 type ships were constructed between 1952 and 1960. Designed for use as either colliers or general cargo ships, several of the type subsequently had their cargo gear removed in order to operate as gearless bulk carriers. The final few vessels were fitted with bipod masts and more modern funnels. Initially registered at Murmansk, in 1975 she was transferred to Zhdanov registry for operation by Azov Shipping Company. She finally arrived at Sveti Kajo, near Split, on 14 October 1985 for breaking. (*Nigel Jones*)

The Azov Shipping Company operated B470 type bulk carrier **Zaporozhye**, built at Gdynia in 1968, transiting the Bosphorus on 3 May 1979 en route from Ho Chi Minh City in Vietnam to a Black Sea port. Ten of the type were built between 1967 and 1971 - the first seven for the Soviet Union followed by three for Poland. Passed in 1992 to Cometas Shipping Company of Mariupol, **Zaporozhye** traded under the same name until 26 December 1996 when, following a voyage in August 1996 from Rouen to Massawa, she was scrapped at Alang. (*John Wiltshire*)

The 1956 Szczecin built B32 type **Chigirin**, also operated by Azov Shipping Company on behalf of the Soviet Union, southbound on 6 May 1979 bound for Genoa. A total of forty-one B32 "Lipetsk" type ships were constructed between 1954 and 1959, with eight sub-types, of which twenty-two were commissioned under the Soviet flag. Poland took nine of the type, the People's Republic of China six, Albania two and Egypt two. **Chigirin**, the fourth of ten ships built in 1955/56 of the second version, finally arrived at Villanueva y Geltru, near Barcelona, on 20 September 1982 for breaking. (*John Wiltshire*)

The 1963 Gdansk built B43 type *Semipalatinsk* northbound on 6 May 1979 during a voyage from Karachi to Odessa. Following a final voyage from Odessa to Da-Nang she was beached at Chittagong on 25 July 1988 for breaking. (*Paul Boot*)

Salavat, the second of seven B43 or Simferopol type ships built at Gdansk in 1962/63, northbound on 24 April 1981 during a voyage from Penang to Ilichevsk. Sold to the Government of Vietnam in 1990, she then traded as *Nezabudka* until beached for scrapping at Calcutta on 24 February 1996. (*Nigel Jones*)

Kapitan Plaushevskiy southbound on 6 May 1979 bound for the Red Sea. A Project 1563 or Slavyansk type (see page 45) built at Kherson in 1970, she was beached at Alang on 7 August 1996. (*John Wiltshire*)

Parizhskaya Kommuna southbound on 18 October 1988 during a voyage from Kherson to Alexandria. She was the last and sole gas-turbine powered ship of the twenty-five strong Project 567 type, developed by the Central Design Bureau "Chernomorsudoproekt" and built at Kherson between 1958 and 1966. At that time, she was the largest gas turbine ship in the world. After being sent to Piraeus in June 1991, her name was shortened to *Parizh* before being beached at Aliaga for scrapping on 16 August 1991. (*Nigel Jones*)

SOVIET SHIPS IN THE BOSPHORUS
SOVIET DANUBE SHIPPING CO.

The 1973 built *Rostok* southbound in July 1983 carrying a part-containerised cargo from her home port of Izmail to Aqaba in Jordan. Constructed by Neptun Werft at Rostock in East Germany, she was the lead ship of a series of eighteen multi-purpose 341 type ships delivered to the Soviet Union between 1973 and 1976. On 2 September 1991, during a voyage from the Soviet Danube port of Reni to Tunis with a cargo of steel coils, *Rostok* developed rudder trouble and was wrecked at mile 31 of the Danube's Sulina Channel, near the Romanian village of Partizani. The final ship of the series, the 1976 built *Rybinsk*, which in 2001 was transferred from Azov Shipping to Ukrainian Danube Shipping Company and renamed *Kapitan Grinenko*, was last seen at Izmail in September 2010. (*David Oldham*)

The 1973 Navashino built *Andrey Kizhevatov* northbound in the Bosphorus on 2 May 1979. She was one of the Sea-River Project 1572 or Kishinev type constructed between 1968 and 1977. On 20 November 1991, *Andrey Kizhevatov* became part of the Ukrainian Danube fleet and was renamed *Danube Voyager*. She was transferred in 2005 to the Sierra Leone flag and sold in 2008 to Ka-Trans Navigation of Odessa. Placed under the Comoros flag and renamed *St.Sophia*, she ran aground in May 2010 and was beached for scrapping at Aliaga on 1 June 2011. (*John Wiltshire*)

The 1972 Constantza built *Sudak* southbound in the Bosphorus on 6 May 1979. She was one of eleven 403/2A or Sosnovets type ships constructed for the Soviet Union by Şantierul Naval Shipyard between 1970 and 1973. Four sister ships were commissioned under the Romanian flag in 1974. On 20 November 1991, *Sudak* became part of the Ukrainian Danube fleet. In 2000 she passed to Ellada Shipping Company of Sevastopol and was provided with passenger accommodation but in 2005 reverted to a pure cargo ship and on 26 December 2011 was beached at Aliaga for breaking. (*John Wiltshire*)

SOVIET SHIPS IN THE BOSPHORUS NOVOROSSIYSK SHIPPING CO.

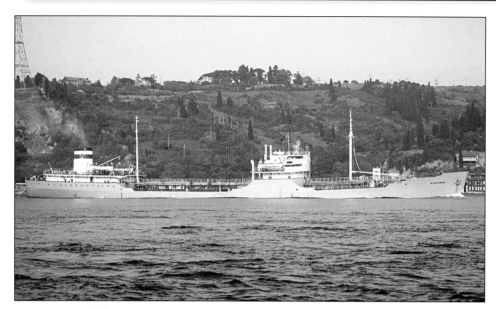

Komsomol, a project 563 type tanker built at Leningrad in 1957, was until 1964 operated on behalf of the Soviet Union by Black Sea Shipping Company and transferred to Novorossisyk Shipping Company in 1967. Photographed southbound on 6 May 1979, she was last reported sailing from Cuba for the Black Sea in April 1984. Then moving to the Far East and operated by Sakhalin Shipping Company, and from 1992 by Vanino Commercial Sea Port, she was scrapped during 1999. (*John Wiltshire*)

Pkhenyan (or *Phenian*), the last of seven Project 573 (Pekin type) tankers constructed at Leningrad by Baltiyskiy Zavod - Baltic Shipbuilding and Engineering Works - between 1959 and 1963, southbound for Trieste on 4 May 1979. Originally allocated by the Directorate of the Soviet Union's oil tanker fleet to Black Sea Shipping Company, she was transferred to Novorossiysk Shipping Company on 20 January 1967. Her name was changed to *Urgut* before sailing from her home port of Novorossisyk in September 1985 bound for Chittagong for breaking. (*John Wiltshire*)

Another of the Soviet Union's Pekin type tankers, the 1960 built *Varshava*, was photographed northbound for the Black Sea from Cuba on 3 June 1981. She was also initially allocated to Black Sea Shipping Company and transferred to Novorossiysk registry in 1967. In March 1984, following a series of voyages from her home port to Genoa, *Varshava* was sent to the Far East and last reported departing from Singapore Roads on 13 April 1984. It is not known where or when she was scrapped but it could have been as late as 1992. (*Dave Salisbury*)

SOVIET UNION SHIPS
LENINSKIY KOMSOMOL TYPE

Valentina Tereshkova, berthed at Montréal on Saturday 7 November 1964, was named after the first woman to go into space - on a solo mission in Vostok 6 on 16 June 1963. The vessel was doubtless flagged out to commemorate the annual parade of new weapons through Red Square in Moscow. Delivered to the Soviet Union on 30 June 1963, she was operated by Black Sea Shipping Company of Odessa. Her name was shortened to *Valentina* for a final loaded voyage from Tuapse to Ube in Japan in August 1988; she was reported as having been scrapped in China during January 1989. (*John Whitehead - René Beauchamp Collection*)

Another of the fast turbine Kherson built project 567 type vessels operated by Black Sea Shipping Company, *Svoboda* was delivered to the Soviet Union on 12 March 1964. She was photographed in Singapore Roads in February 1980 during a voyage from Tobata in Japan to her home port of Odessa. She served the Soviet Union until sold to Bangladesh breakers, being beached at Chittagong on 16 July 1989. (*Ian Shiffman*)

SOVIET UNION SHIPS ICE STRENGTHENED

The Murmansk registered *Lena*, photographed in the St. Lawrence River passing Verchères eastbound on 2 August 1981, was the first of a series of six diesel-electric engined ships built at Flushing in Holland between 1954 and 1957 for Polar service. Her sister ships were named *Ob*, *Yenisey* (or *Enisey*), *Angara* (allocated to Far-Eastern Shipping Company), *Indigirka* and *Baykal* (operated by the Northern Fleet of the Soviet Navy as *OC-30* until wrecked in December 1978). The last reported voyage of *Lena* was sailing from Antwerp on 1 July 1982 bound for Murmansk, following which she was sold to Spanish breakers at San Esteban de Pravia, work commencing on 4 July 1983. (*Marc Piché*)

The 1971 Kherson built *Pavel Ponomaryev* passing Varennes, on the south shore of the St.Lawrence River across from Montréal-Nord, on 12 February 1982 bound for her home port of Murmansk. The photographer advises that he had photographed the ship from atop a grain drying facility alongside the river, necessitating a climb of several flights of stairs and a 50-foot high ladder to reach the top. *Pavel Ponomaryev* was the penultimate ship in a type 550 series of thirteen ships built between 1962 and 1972, of which the first ten were constructed at Komsomolsk and the final three, built at Kherson, an improved version. These were followed in 1975 by *Mikhail Somov*, delivered to the Soviet Navy as a polar research ship. *Pavel Ponomaryev* was beached for scrapping at Alang on 8 February 1995. (*Marc Piché*)

The 1957 Nikolayev built *Rionges* sailing from Cardiff on 2 August 1974 during a voyage from Saint John, New Brunswick to her home port of Murmansk via London, Cardiff and Antwerp. She was the third of six Project 564 vessels constructed by the Ivan Nosenko Shipbuilding Yard in 1956/57. Her sister ships, named *Dneproges*, *Volkhovges*, *Angarges*, *Kuybyshevges* and *Tsimlyanskges*, were also allocated to Murmansk Shipping Company. After idling at Murmansk for much of 1976, *Rionges* arrived at Castellon breakers on 3 December 1976. Her sister ships were all scrapped during 1977/78. (*John Wiltshire*)

SOVIET UNION SHIPS ROSTOCK BUILT

Povenets, delivered to the Soviet Union in May 1963 and allocated to Estonia, was the lead ship of a forty strong series built by Neptun Werft at Rostock in East Germany. Of these, only the 1963-built *Povenets*, *Pyarnu*, *Novovoronezh* and *Pereslavl-Zalesskiy* were equipped with goalpost style masts. All others, including the 1963-built *Gorno-Altaysk*, *Kypu*, *Ristna* and *Gzhatsk* were given two bipod masts. *Povenets* was photographed from the eastern bank of the Manchester Ship Canal at Eastham inbound for Ellesmere Port on 7 August 1988 during a voyage from Kaliningrad via Grangemouth. On 21 April 1992, following her sale to Dodge Shipping of Piraeus, she sailed from Tallinn bound for Piraeus where she was renamed *Joy Alfa*. She was beached for scrapping at Alang on 5 July 1993. (*Author*)

Sister ship *Vilyany*, delivered at Rostock in October 1964 and also allocated to Estonia, was photographed sailing past Eastham ferry on 9 May 1991 outbound from Ellesmere Port on the Manchester Ship Canal following discharge of a cargo from Kaliningrad. Renamed *Tootsi* in 1992, she was sold in 1994 to Trex Shipping of Odessa, a company which also had an office in Dublin. Renamed *Lada*, flying the Russian flag, she briefly traded in the Far East before being beached at Calcutta on 29 September 1995 for breaking. (*Author*)

The 1959 Rostock built *Loksa*, a Project 251 or Andizhan type, photographed in November 1981, was initially operated on behalf of the Soviet Union by Latvian State Shipping Company, from 1967 by Estonia State Shipping Company. Approximately fifty ships of this type were delivered by Neptun Werft to the Soviet Union between 1958 and 1962. Three of the final ships of the type were built as the cadet training ships *Gorizont*, *Zenit* and *Meridian*. *Loksa* finally arrived for scrapping at Vigo on 16 May 1986. (*Author's collection*)

SOVIET UNION SHIPS WARNEMÜNDE BUILT

The 1970 Warnemünde built **Ilya Ulyanov** passing Terneuzen on 25 May 1986 inbound for Antwerp during a voyage from Leningrad to Acajutla, El Salvador. Following the end of the Soviet Union, Baltic Shipping Company continued to trade the ship until her transfer early in 1997 into the management of the linked Pan Oceanic of London. Renamed **Ocean Falcon**, she finally sailed from Suez on 26 June 1997 for Assab before being beached at Chittagong on 30 August 1997 for breaking. (*Simon Olsen*)

The Mercator type **Walter Ulbricht**, named after the leader of East Germany until 1971, was delivered to the Soviet Union at Warnemünde, near Rostock, on 7 May 1974. Photographed in the River Mersey departing from Gladstone Lock, Liverpool, on 23 November 1991, she was then employed on a regular service to East Africa. Given the Russian name **Priozersk** in 1992, she served Baltic Shipping Company until 1997 when she was transferred to the Moscow based AO Sovfracht. Her name shortened to **Ozersk**, she finally arrived for scrap at Alang on 15 December 2000. (*Author*)

SOVIET UNION SHIPS HUNGARIAN BUILT

The Tallinn registered Spartak type **August Kulberg**, built at Budapest in 1969, approaching Eastham Locks, Manchester Ship Canal, on 24 January 1988. Renamed **Pakri** by Estonia in 1991, she was sold in 1997 to the locally based Rein Merisalu's Baltic Group International to become **Alvina M.** and in 2001 resold to Nargen Maritime Agency to trade as **Yana E.** until sent to Alang for breaking, being beached on 12 February 2006. (*Author*)

The Archangel registered **Kondratiy Bulavin**, also built at Budapest in 1969, outbound from Eastham on 11 April 1988. In 1995 she was sold to Nesco of Estonia to trade as **Sky Vine** but in 1997 was renamed **Krookus** before sailing later in the year for the Far East to trade for new owners as **Nat Star**, then from 2002 as **Sea Line** and from 2004 as **Arsenal**, finally arriving at Tianjin for scrap on 21 June 2009. (*Author*)

Ivan Goncharov in the St.Lawrence River at Montréal on 17 June 1982 eastbound from Hamilton, Ontario, her hull bearing the joint service name "Sovindship". One of the B44 Murom type, built at Gdansk in 1966, she was operated by Black Sea Shipping Company until sold late in 1991 to the Vietnam government. Renamed Lily, she reverted to the Ukrainian flag while at Nikolayev in late 1995 and finally arrived for scrapping at Alang on 11 November 1996. (*René Beauchamp*)

The 1968 Gdansk built B40 type *Ignatiy Sergeyev* (or *Sergeev*), operated by Black Sea Shipping Company, berthed at Southampton in April 1975. She was in port for one week from 4 April 1975 during a voyage from Wismar to Havana. On 18 October 1996, soon after being transferred to the Ukrainian Shipping Company of Odessa, she collided with a dredger on arrival at Kakinada in India, was arrested and beached on 24 June 1998, subsequently being broken up "in situ". (*Author's Collection*)

Northern Shipping Company of Archangel's 1965 Gdansk built B45 **Naryan-Mar** in the River Mersey approaching Gladstone Lock, Liverpool, from Tallinn on 26 May 1990. She subsequently spent much of 1990 under repair at her home port of Archangel before sailing from Caen on 9 December bound for Toamasina in Madagascar, never to return home. She was beached for scrapping at Alang on 12 October 1991 under the St.Vincent & Grenadines flag, having meanwhile been sold to the London based intermediaries Incom Ltd. (*Author*)

Baltic Shipping Company (BSC)'s Leningrad registered **Dvinoles**, a B514 or Volgoles type (see page 16) built at Gdansk in 1960, berthed at Aberdeen in May 1976. A total of sixteen ships of that type were built by Stocznia Gdanska for the Soviet Union between 1960 and 1962, with ten operated by BSC, two by Northern Shipping Company and four by Far-Eastern Shipping Company. They were followed by sixty-six similar ships of the B45 or Belomorskles type. BSC continued to trade **Dvinoles** until sending her to Alang for breaking, where she was beached on 30 September 1994. (*Alastair Paterson*)

The Admiral Makarov High School of Marine Engineers of Leningrad's B80 type cadet training ship **Professor Shchegolev** arriving at Cardiff on 6 September 1971. She was the second of a series of nine Szczecin built ships given "Professor" names delivered to the Soviet Union between 1970 and 1973. Two similar ships were retained by Poland, another was delivered to Bulgaria and one was also delivered to Romania. In 1992 the management of **Professor Shchegolev** was placed with Baltic Shipping Company and in 1996 she was transferred to Novorossiysk Marine Academy. On 4 May 2007 she was beached for scrapping at Aliaga as **Krita**. (*John Wiltshire*)

SOVIET UNION SHIPS FINNISH BUILT

The 1957 built *Kirovsk*, an example of the ten "Archangelsk" type of the Equator class constructed by Wärtsilä Crichton-Vulcan at Turku, was operated by Baltic Shipping Company of Leningrad. She was photographed transiting the Great Lakes in September 1969. The final voyage of *Kirovsk* commenced from Gdynia on 3 September 1984 bound for Hŭngnam in North Korea. Reportedly scrapped in 1985 at a port in the U.S.S.R., this must therefore have been in the Far East. (*Author's Collection*)

The 1963 Turku built *Izhevskles* was photographed off Cardiff on 9 August 1982, from her stern tug, on arrival from her home port of Archangelsk with a cargo of timber. In 1993 she was one of many ships transferred by Northern Shipping Company into the management of Unimar of Greece and renamed *Blaze*. However, in 1995 she was sold to Syria and renamed *Shaher M.*, then quickly resold to Turkey to trade as *Furkan*. Renamed *Kros Istanbul* in 2002, and becoming *Gnocchi* from 2004, her name was abbreviated to *Occhi* before being beached at Aliaga on 20 September 2006 for breaking. (*John Wiltshire*)

Novovyatsk, one of the final ships of the Novgorod type, built at Turku in 1970 and operated on behalf of the Soviet Union by Baltic Shipping Company, outbound from Vancouver in April 1988. In 1995 she briefly joined the linked Balt-Med fleet as *Mirto* before being sold in 1996 to Shipshape Maritime Corporation (Citi Shipping, Mumbai). Managed by Crossseas Shipping of Leicester and renamed *Citi Breeze*, on 6 March 1988 she was arrested at Colombo due to an alleged outstanding mortgage settlement. From there she proceeded to Alang for scrapping and was beached on 21 September 1998. (*Ray Thorsteinson*)

The 1983 Rauma built tanker *Ventspils*, managed on behalf of the Soviet Union by Latvian Shipping Company, arriving at Barry on 25 November 1989, probably with a cargo of molasses. Flagged out from 1995, she was sold in 1999 to the Russian Inspector's & Marine Surveyors' Corporation (RIMSCO) of Vladivostok and reportedly scrapped in China during July 2016. (*John Wiltshire*)

Following discharge at Liverpool of a cargo from Leningrad, *Vytegra* is seen departing on 9 May 1991 bound for Blaye in France to load a cargo of grain for Klaipeda. One of the Russian built Project 596M type, constructed at Vyborg in 1967 to the Leningrad built Vytegrales design, she was operated by Northern Shipping Company until September 1991. Then departing from Archangel for La Spezia, Unimar soon assumed her management. Renamed *Rita D*, she traded as such until 1996 when she was sold to Jamal Suleiman Chehram of Lattakia, Syria, and renamed *Zizi*. On 18 July 2000, then owned by the Larnaca based Nova Star Trading, she sailed from there for India as *Stamy Waves II*. Having left Suez under tow on 11 August 2000, she was beached for scrapping at Calcutta on 3 November 2000. (*Author*)

The 1970 built *Pamir*, one of a second series of Project 596M type ships constructed at Vyborg between 1965 and 1972, was photographed berthed in King George Dock, Hull, in August 1983 alongside the 1965 built *Sangarles*, one of the first 596M series. *Pamir* had arrived from Igarka on 18 August, sailing on 31 August for Leningrad, while *Sangarles* had earlier arrived from Archangel and soon departed for Bremen. In 1991 *Pamir* was one of the first ships transferred by Northern Shipping Company into the management of Unimar of Greece. Renamed *Uniarch*, in 1995 she was sold to Ali Sahyouni of Lattakia, Syria, to trade as *Bassel* until beached at Alang on 8 October 2000 for breaking; *Sangarles* was scrapped in 1987.(*Author's Collection*)

The 1973 Kherson built Dnepr type *Geroi Panfilovtsy*, employed on the Soviet Union's Odessa Ocean Line container service, departing from Karachi on 3 March 1983 during a voyage from Ilyichevsk to Bangkok. In late 1998, when one of the last remaining ships in the BLASCO fleet, she was sold to clients of Black Sea Transport of Istanbul and renamed *Anatolia Sun*. In mid 1999 she was further renamed *Gerta*, managed by Rotos Shipping & Transport Agency of Hamburg, possibly acting as ship breaking intermediaries. *Gerta* disappeared, presumably scrapped, after sailing from Port Sudan on 17 September 1999. (*Bryan Shankland*)

The 1970 Vyborg built **Vyborgskaya Storona**, operated by Northern Shipping Company, passing Eastham Ferry inbound for the Manchester Ship Canal on 8 April 1990. In 1998 she was sold to Penta Maritime of Tallinn to trade as **Timber Star**, as which she sailed for the Far East in mid 2000. Resold in 2003 to Golden Pride Co. Ltd. of Nakhodka, Russia, she remained in the Far East until sold for scrap on 16 May 2010. (*Author*)

The Leningrad registered **Ivan Derbenev** was a locally built project 1607 or "Neva" type ro/ro, delivered to Baltic Shipping Company in 1978. Photographed in the Welland Canal on 25 April 1988, she was transferred in 1996 to the Russian Government owned Altex Shipping Company of St.Petersburg. Renamed **Delfshaven** in 1999 for a charter to Van Uden Maritime of Rotterdam, she was beached at Alang on 22 May 2001 for breaking. (*Jeff Cameron*)

The 37,500 grt, 263 metre long and 32 metre wide, barge carrier **Le Duan**, completed at Kherson on 30 June 1987, was equipped with two diesel engines giving her a service speed of 18 knots. Photographed at Singapore on 4 October 1987, on her maiden voyage to Vietnam, she and her two sister ships subsequently became units of the BLASCO fleet but served only until 1995. After the collapse of the Soviet Union, Vietsovlighter (VSL, the manager of the three ships) and BLASCO experienced great difficulties with securing sufficient inbound cargo to Vietnam. **Le Duan** idled under arrest at Rotterdam from 22 May 1995 until sold in June 1997 to the same United States buyers who bought sister ship **Ernesto Che Guevara**. She had idled at Odessa from 8 February 1996 until sailing in April 1997 for Vũng Tàu in Vietnam as **Gaysin**, managed by Ukline, a new BLASCO subsidiary. There, as USD 162,000 was owed to the port authorities, she was detained for over two months. The third ship **Indira Gandhi** was arrested following her arrival in Suez Bay on 28 August 1995 and, after a final voyage to Haiphong one year later, idled under repair at Ilyichevsk from 12 October 1996 until August 1998 when sold and renamed **Quan Yin**, as which she proceeded to Pakistan for breaking in April 1999. (*Simon Olsen*)

SOVIET UNION SHIPS
TANKERS

Built by the Brodogradilište III Maj shipyard at Rijeka, Yugoslavia, **Pablo Neruda** was the lead ship of a series of eleven tankers built for the Soviet Union between 1975 and 1979 and operated by Latvian Shipping Company. **Pablo Neruda** is seen in the River Elbe passing Cuxhaven eastbound in August 1987. Although flagged out from 1998, the vessel continued to be owned by Latvia until beached at Chittagong on 9 October 2003 for breaking. Her Latvian sister ship **Pols Robsons** (built as **Paul Robeson**) was renamed **Pablo Neruda** in 2004, trading as such until scrapped at Chittagong in February 2007. (*Gerhard Fiebiger*)

Groznyy was an early example of thirty-three Project 563 type tankers constructed at Kherson between 1953 and 1961. She was operated on behalf of the Soviet Union by Black Sea Shipping Company until 1966 and thereafter by Novorossiysk Shipping Company until 1975. She was then converted at Vladivostok in 1975 for use as a gas storage tanker and bunker base at Nakhodka. **Groznyy** was photographed in Singapore Roads on 4 October 1990 en route to breakers at Karachi. (*Simon Olsen*)

The Skaramanga built tanker **Urzhum** was delivered to the Soviet Union on 20 January 1983 for operation by Novorossiysk Shipping Company. She was the last of five identical tankers constructed by Hellenic Shipyard in 1982/83 for operation from the U.S.S.R.'s Novorossiysk Black Sea port. Another five ships of the type, commencing with **World Process**, were delivered between 1984 and 1986 to the Greek owner Niarchos. **Urzhum** was photographed passing Gravesend on 4 December 1983. After nine years flagged out to Cyprus from 1990, she was sold to Morfini S.r.L of Bari, Italy, to trade as **Siren** until sold to Indonesia in 2005 and renamed **Sukses XI**. She was beached at Chittagong for scrapping on 28 January 2015 as **Hua Hui**. (*Simon Olsen*)

SOVIET UNION SHIPS
SOVIET FIRSTS

Slavyansk, the lead ship of the 17 knot project 1563 type built at Kherson, fitted with a diesel engine and two five tonne cranes with open lattice-style jibs, arriving at Liverpool from Qingdao on 11 November 1986 with a cargo of cottonseed and rapeseed. Delivered to the Soviet Union on 31 December 1966, Black Sea Shipping Company operated the vessel until her sale to Alang breakers, where she was beached on 5 June 1997. (*Brian Fisher*)

Sovfracht, the first vessel operated by Sovcomflot, albeit managed by Black Sea Shipping Company, passing Québec City on 8 August 1990 during a voyage from Sorel to Nikolayev with a cargo of grain. Built at Rijeka in 1967 as *Saara Aarnio* for a Finnish owner, on acquisition by the Soviet Union early in 1973 she was initially named *Magdi* but quickly took the name *Sovfracht* (or *Sovfrakht*). Sold in October 1990 to Stanship Inc. of New York and Athens, she traded as *Delta Trident* until beached at Alang on 23 July 1997 for breaking. (*Simon Olsen Collection*)

The 1968 Gdansk built B40 type **Bela Kun** swinging in the River Mersey on 2 September 1994, shortly after departing from Langton Lock, Liverpool, bound for Riga. She had discharged at Liverpool a cargo of oilseed for the manufacture of animal feedstuffs (AFS). A total of sixteen B40 or Kommunist type ships were delivered to the Soviet Union by Stocznia Gdanska between 1968 and 1970 while another four were built at Szczecin. All but one of the B40 type were allocated to Black Sea Shipping Company. The exception was **Kho Chi Minh** (or **Ho Chi Minh**), delivered into the management of Far-Eastern Shipping Company. In 1996 one of the Ukrainian ships, **Fridrikh Engels**, was transferred to Mykolayiv (Nikolayev) Commercial Sea Port to trade as **Mykola Movchan**, as which she survived until September 2000. **Bela Kun** was beached for scrapping at Alang on 12 February 1997. (*Author*)

The 1967 Kherson built, Project 1563 type, **Sochi** departing from Langton Lock, Liverpool, on 1 May 1994 following discharge of a cargo of rice bran from Kakinada in India, again for use in the manufacture of AFS. **Sochi** was the second in a series of thirty-one vessels delivered to the Soviet Union for operation by Black Sea Shipping Company between 1966 and 1973, the lead ship being **Slavyansk** (see page 45). The final ten ships were fitted with a 60-ton heavy-lift derrick. In November 1997 **Sochi** was sold to Asia Express Shipping of Dubai, briefly trading as **Mashraq I** before being sold to Indian breakers and beached at Alang on 24 April 1998. (*Author*)

The 1968 Warnemünde built **Izmail** arriving at Birkenhead on 10 March 1995 from India via Lorient with a cargo of rice bran. She was the second in a series of twenty-six vessels delivered to the Soviet Union between 1968 and 1972, the lead ship being **Irkutsk**. Only the first three ships of the type were allocated to Black Sea Shipping Company, most of the remainder, including the last fourteen of a modified design incorporating a 60-ton heavy-lift derrick, joining Baltic Shipping Company. Transferred in July 1996 to a new organisation named Ukrainian Shipping Company, which was created in 1992 and managed by Tor Shipping Ltd of Odessa, *Izmail* was arrested at Colombo in May 1997 and finally sailed for Chittagong in July 1998, being beached for scrapping on 8 January 1999. (*Author*)

The 1968 Gdansk built B40 type **Jeanne Labourbe** (or **Zhanna Lyaburb**) arriving at Immingham on 24 April 1997 with a cargo of oilseed for the manufacture of animal feedstuffs. This was her final loaded voyage for Black Sea Shipping Company; she had earlier been reported sailing from Penang on 6 January 1997 bound for the Philippine port of Gingoog. She was then sold to breaking intermediaries Transmarine Shipping & Trading of Hamburg, sailing under the shortened name of **Jeanne** to Myanmar via Larnaca, en route lightly grounding in the Suez Canal on 6 July 1997. She was beached at Alang for scrapping on 4 September 1997. (*Author*)

The 1965 Pula, Yugoslavia, built **Nazym Khikmet** approaching Avonmouth on 5 December 1992 with a cargo of rice bran. She was one of twenty ships delivered to the Soviet Union by the Brodogradilište "Uljanik" shipyard between 1964 and 1971, the lead ship appropriately being named **Pula**. Whereas the first thirteen ships were allocated to Black Sea Shipping Company, the final seven were allocated to Far-Eastern Shipping Company, with four of those being converted to container ships in 1979. Another series of ten ships of the Pula type was built for the Soviet Union between 1967 and 1970 by the Brodogradilište III Maj shipyard at Rijeka. **Nazym Khikmet** was beached for scrapping at Chittagong on 10 February 1997. (*Author*)

The iconic Ukraine seafarer training ship **Lesozavodsk**, commissioned by the Soviet Union in December 1960 for operation by Black Sea Shipping Company, had been withdrawn from commercial service in June 1983 following a final voyage from Cuba to Odessa. She was one of twenty-nine B54 type ships built at Gdansk between 1956 and 1963, of which seven were delivered to the Soviet Union between 1958 and 1960. These were followed in 1961 by a further two ships of the similar B541 type, **Divnogorsk** (see page 16) and **Mednogorsk**, built at Szczecin. Between 1984 and 1991 **Lesozavodsk** was converted at the Ilyichevsk Shipyard for use at Odessa as a simulator training centre, with her main engine dismantled. This photograph shows her condition on 16 March 2012, when still actively employed in that role. (*Vladimir Lemonos*)

The 1968 Kherson built, project 1563 type, **Vega** berthed at Malaga on 10 September 1993 loading a cargo for Cuba. After serving the Soviet Union as **Komsomolskaya Slava** it was decided in 1993 to give her the simpler, less Russian name of **Vega**, painting her funnel in colours based upon the Ukraine flag. Similar action was taken with two other ships, renamed **Deneb** and **Sirius**. Following a voyage from Odessa to Ho Chi Minh City in October 1996, **Vega** proceeded to Alang for scrap, being beached on 17 April 1997. (*Andrew Wiltshire*)

The 1965 Gdansk built B44 type **Mezhdurechensk** in Singapore Roads on 16 April 1993 during a voyage to Odessa. Between 1963 and 1967, a total of twenty-nine ships of the B44 or Murom type, including seven built at Szczecin, were delivered to the Soviet Union. In 1991, **Mezhdurechensk** was one of ten ships allocated by Black Sea Shipping Company to the Vietsovlighter ("VSL") joint venture with Vietnam, although the letters VSL were not painted on her funnel at that time. Following a final call at Odessa in July 1996, she sailed from Inchon in December 1996 bound for China and from there proceeded to Mongla in Bangladesh. She was beached at Alang on 13 March 1997 for scrapping. (*Gerhard Fiebiger*)

The ocean-going UT 505 type tug **Zubr** was built in 1977 at Hjelset, and completed at nearby Ulsteinvik on the west coast of Norway, as **Biscay Sky** for Biscayan Towage & Salvage, an operation owned by Ramon de la Sota of Bilbao. Together with sister tug **Biscay Star**, renamed **Bizon**, she was acquired by the Soviet Union in 1979 for operation by Black Sea Shipping Company. **Zubr** is seen in West Float, Birkenhead, taking on bunkers from **Taffgarth** (the former **Contractor**, ex **Regent Wren**) on 22 December 1996 ahead of towing the Nigerian ship **River Andoni** to Aliaga for breaking. Both tugs were sold to Italy in 1998, **Zubr** becoming **Mascalzone Oceanico**. Since 2009 she has operated as **Ionion Pelagos** and was last reported at Piraeus in 2020. **Bizon** was last reported at Lagos in 2019 as **Janni**. (*Author*)

Azov Shipping Company's 1984 Kherson built *Ivan Pereverzev* berthed in Liverpool's Gladstone Dock on 9 January 1999. The last of the successful Project 1585 or Dnepr type to be built for the Soviet Union, she was renamed *Shakhtar* in 2001 and transferred in 2003 to Commercial Fleet of Donbass. Her name was shortened to *Akhtar* for her scrap voyage to Chittagong where she was beached on 3 May 2011. The first ship of the Dnepr type, named after the river on which the Kherson shipyard is situated, was *Geroi Panfilovtsy* (see page 42), delivered in February 1973 for operation by Black Sea Shipping Company, to which the majority of the type built for the U.S.S.R. was allocated. In December 1976, the Liverpool based Ocean Transport & Trading took delivery of two of the 1585E version, named *Laertes* and *Lycaon*. (*Author*)

Kapitan Papkov berthed in Liverpool's Canada Dock on 8 May 1997 loading cargo for Apapa/ Lagos. She was one of thirty-six Zhdanov Project 426 or "Komsomol" type ships built at Leningrad between 1968 and 1975, the design having been developed in the Central Design Bureau "Baltsudoproekt". She was delivered to the Soviet Union in August 1974 as *Leninskiye Iskry*, assigned to Azov Shipping Company; she was renamed *Kapitan Papkov* in 1995. Sold in 1998 to Ashapura Shipping of Mumbai, she then traded as *Arab Glory* until beached for scrapping at her home port on 25 May 2002. The series was named "Komsomol" to commemorate the fiftieth anniversary of the creation in 1918 of the All-Union Leninist Young Communist League (or VLKSM). A further nine ships of the type were built in Egypt between 1974 and 1982. (*Author*)

The Rostock built, Neptun 471 type, *Kramatorsk* entering Langton Lock outbound from Liverpool on 12 September 1998. Delivered to Bernhard Schulte in February 1980 as *Wellwood*, from October 1984 to June 1985 she traded as *Goodwood*, managed by Hanseatic of Limassol. She was then purchased by Azov Shipping Company and renamed *Kramatorsk*. However, between December 1999 and January 2003 she was managed by Westmar Shipping Ltd of Piraeus as *Kristine*. In January 2003 her ownership was transferred to Commercial Fleet of Donbass as *Kramatorsk*. In September 2010 she was renamed *Mayank*, and placed under the flag of Georgia, but was beached at Mumbai on 19 August 2011 for breaking. (*Author*)

UKRAINE SHIPS
GULF AZOV SHIPPING COMPANY

The 1966 Gdansk built **Dubai Success**, the former **Samuil Marshak**, was photographed berthed at Mina Qaboos on 12 October 1991, shortly after her transfer from Black Sea Shipping Company to Gulf Azov Shipping Company. **Dubai Success** was beached for scrapping at Alang on 31 July 1996. (*Hans Hoffmann*)

GASCO's 1978 Warnemünde built **Dubai Valour**, the former **Jalamudra** purchased from Scindia in 1995, arriving at Durban on 3 July 1997 during a voyage from Kandla to Sapele. On arrival there she idled for many months, was arrested on 30 April 1998 and later renamed **Grace**. She then returned to Mariupol, sailing on 22 July 1999 for India. In 2001 she was sold to Oasis Maritime Services of Dubai. Renamed **Strength** early in 2002, she was beached at Alang on 27 July 2002 for breaking. (*Trevor Jones*)

UKRAINE SHIPS
COMETAS & UKRAINIAN DANUBE

Cometas Shipping of Mariupol, a subsidiary of Azov Shipping Company, operated a total of seven ships at various stages between 1991 and 2010. The 1972 Bremerhaven built 36-L type **Cometas** was photographed departing from Birkenhead on 25 May 2001 following discharge of a cargo of timber from Belem. The former **Manley Falmouth**, built as **Araluck** for Hilmar Reksten, she had been transferred to Cometas in 1996 following the similar **Azovlloyd** (the former **Manley Devon**, ex **Nedlloyd Nile**), **Manley Exeter** (ex **Nedlloyd Niger**) and **Mariupol Star** (the former **Manley Gosport**, ex **Gordian**) in 1994/5.

Azovlloyd remained in the fleet only until the end of 1996, **Manley Exeter** until 1999 and **Mariupol Star** until 2001, **Cometas** finally arrived off Alang on 1 September 2002 for scrapping. (*Author*)

Ukrainian Danube Shipping Company of Izmail's **Ilya Selvinskiy**, built in 1975 at Navashino (Oka River, Russia) for the Soviet Danube Shipping Company and taken into Ukrainian ownership in 1992, was photographed departing from Port-Saint-Louis-du-Rhône, near Fos-Marseille, on 27 October 2001 with a cargo of grain. The vessel's current whereabouts and situation are unknown. (*Author*)

UKRAINE SHIPS CRIMEA BASED

Tkvarcheli, a fish factory trawler built at Flushing in 1968, departing from Liverpool on 26 July 1996 when in Ukrainian colours. In October 1950, the Soviet Union's Ministry of Fishing Industry had established a fishery and sealing base at the port of Kerch on the eastern shores of Kerch Bay in eastern Crimea, on the Sea of Azov, utilising a fleet of small vessels. *Tkvarcheli*'s manager, KPORP "Kerchrybprom", was failing when she was sent to Aliaga in June 2004 for scrapping. (*Author*)

The 1985 Rousse (Bulgaria) built vegetable oil tanker *Tamanskiy*, owned by the Ukrainian state and also operated by Kerchrybprom, passing Porto Corsini, outbound from Ravenna, early on 17 May 2002. In December 2015 it was reported that the vessel, then berthed at Yalova in Turkey, had been stolen but by January 2019 she was owned by Servis State Enterprise of Kiev. In July 2022 *Tamanskiy* was reported berthed at Chornomorsk. (*Author*)

The Ukrainian owned vegetable oil tankers *Vostochnyy* and *Yuzhnyy*, respectively built for the Soviet Union at Rousse in 1988 and 1984, are seen laid up at Sevastopol on 3 February 2014. Operated during the Soviet era by Sevastopol sea fishing port (SPORP "Atlantika"), both ships were transferred to Chornomorsk fishing port in 2014. *Vostochnyy* (which was named *Mela* between 2014 and 2018) was moved on 18 February 2022 from Chornomorsk to Mykolaiv, where she was trapped. *Yuzhnyy*, which was named *Manganary* until 1997 and since 2014 has operated as *Pata*, has been idle at Chornomorsk since 2017. (*Evgeniy Belichenko*)

Yeyskiy Liman, a fish carrier constructed at Hamburg in 1968 as the reefer *Sloman Alsterpark* and modified following acquisition by the Soviet Union in 1975, passing Terneuzen inbound for Antwerp on 8 April 1995. Until 1987 she was operated by Mortransflot of Kaliningrad but, as that organisation was then closed, she was moved to Sevastopol for operation by Yugrybkholodfrlot, and later by Yugryba. *Yeyskiy Liman* was beached at Bombay on 27 July 1995 for breaking. (*Simon Olsen*)

UKRAINE SHIPS
OTHER UKRAINIAN COMPANIES

The London based agency Blasco U.K. Limited became Ocean Agencies Limited in 1996 and, working closely with Strongtec Systems and Sudoservice of Odessa, assumed the management and eventual disposal of six former Black Sea Shipping Company vessels, given the names *Irene 1* to *6*. The 1967 Nikolayev built *Irene 1*, the former *Kapitan Kushnarenko*, was photographed discharging a cargo of rice bran at Newport on 8 February 1997. She was then sent directly to Alang for scrapping. It is noteworthy that she was the first of the twenty-two ships of the Project 1568 series built between 1967 and 1975 for operation by Black Sea Shipping Company. Nine more ships, of the 1568E type, were delivered to foreign owners while another was delivered in 1970 to the U.S.S.R.'s Academy of Sciences as the research vessel *Akademik Sergei Korolev*, confirming the good tactical and technical characteristics of the *Kapitan Kushnarenko* dry-cargo hulls. (*Author*)

St. Luke, operated by Ukmar on behalf of BLASCO , in Singapore's eastern anchorage on 31 July 2002 prior to sailing for Pohang with a cargo of scrap metal loaded at Liverpool. One of the fourteen strong Khariton Greku series of bulk carriers built for the Soviet Union by the Okean Shipyard at Oktyabrskoye, Nikolayev, she was delivered on 1 December 1984 as *Nikolay Kuznetsov* for operation by Black Sea Shipping Company. In mid 1996 she was flagged out to Liberia and renamed *Altestovo*, managed from London by Ocean Agencies Ltd. In 1997, she was reflagged to Malta and early in 1999 became *St. Luke*. Following a voyage in January 2003 to Inchon in Taiwan, she was sold to Far East Hainan Shipping and, managed from Qinhuangdao, traded locally as *Da Ye* until scrapped at Zhangjiagang in August 2012. (*Roger Hurcombe*)

St. Anna, managed on behalf of BLASCO by Staff Centre Ship Management of Odessa, swinging in the River Mersey on departure from Gladstone Lock, Liverpool, on 2 May 2008. Another of the Khariton Greku series of bulk carriers built for the Soviet Union by the Okean Shipyard at Oktyabrskoye, Nikolayev, she was delivered in June 1986 as *Akademik Blagonravov*. In 1996 the Black Sea Shipping Company renamed her *Akkerman*, managed by Ocean Agencies Ltd. In 1998 she became *St. George*, now managed by Ukmar. In 2006 Staff Centre Ship Management took control of the vessel, renaming her *St. Anna*, and she finally arrived off Alang for scrapping on 22nd September 2011. (*Author*)

The 1983 Perm (Russia) built ore/oil carrier *Nefterudovoz-45M*, owned by TBS Shipping Company of Kherson, in the City cargo area of Dnipro river port on 29 July 2019. Built for use by Volgotanker River Shipping Company of Astrakhan, she was one of two identical ships which in 2014 were sold to Ukraine by Volgotrans LLC of Samara, Russia. She continues to trade in the Black Sea and River Danube. (*Maksym Pysmennyi*)

The Yevpatoriya, Crimea, registered, 1995 Kiev built, *Vomv-Gaz* photographed from Porto Corsini, opposite Marina di Ravenna, inbound on 4 June 2001. In 2006 *Vomv-Gaz* was reflagged in Malta, nominally owned by Getpoint Shipping Ltd and managed by Maloye Predpriyatiye 'Meridian' of Odessa, but was hulked in 2007. (*Author*)

UKRAINE SHIPS
KAALBYE SHIPPING

Galina II was photographed berthing in Canada Dock, Liverpool, on 13 October 1997 on arrival to load a break-bulk cargo for Apapa/Lagos. She was built for the Soviet Union at Nikolayev in 1975 as *Kapitan Slipko* and operated by Black Sea Shipping Company until purchased by Kaalbye Shipping at Odessa in June 1997. Following a final voyage from Ilichevsk to Bandar Abbas in April 2000, *Galina II* was sold to breakers at Mumbai where she was beached on 23rd May 2000. (*Author*)

Kaalbye Shipping's *Julia IV* passing Rozenburg, inbound for Rotterdam, in May 1998. She was built for the Soviet Union at Nikolayev in 1974 as *Kapitan Georgiy Baglay* and operated by Black Sea Shipping Company until sold to Kaalbye in June 1997. *Julia IV* finally arrived at Alang on 19 August 2000 to be scrapped. (*Author's Collection*)

Kaalbye Shipping's 1975 Nikolayev built **Sumy** gliding past Portishead outbound from Portbury Dock near Avonmouth on 20 April 2000 on her last voyage to North Europe, bound for Rotterdam with a part cargo of forest products from the Far East. Built for the Soviet Union as **Kapitan Leontiy Borisyenko**, and capable of 18.5 knots when new, Black Sea Shipping Company had sold her to Kaalbye early in 1998. With the management involvement of Sudoservice of Odessa, she sailed under the flag of St.Vincent & The Grenadines, registered at Kingstown, until finally beached at Alang for scrapping on 13 September 2000. (*Author*)

The 1983 Kherson built **Lady Juliet** passing Portishead on 2 July 2004 inbound for Portbury Dock with a cargo of forest products from the Far East. Delivered to Beogradska Plovidba of Yugoslavia as **Kapetan Pavlović**, she had been sold in 1991 to Baru Seri Inc. of Piraeus to trade as **Runner B.**, briefly renamed **Afris Runner** in 1996/7 for a charter, until sold to Kaalbye Shipping early in 2001. She was beached at Alang on 2 July 2011 for breaking. (*Author*)

The 1976 Bremer Vulkan, Vegesack, built **Lady Juliet** at Dunkirk in May 1999. She subsequently sailed from Odessa on 28 June 1999 for Haiphong and continued trading until beached at Chittagong on 9 November 2000 for breaking. Delivered to Ellerman Lines in September 1976 as **City of Canterbury**, financed by Barclays Bank, she was sold in 1981 to Architug Shipping S.A. (Miltiadis Karagiannakis) of Athens to trade as **Arc Aeolos** until sold to Nine Paulsen of Oslo in May 1989. Then named **Sletter**, she was however immediately chartered out as **Nortween Sletter**, and then briefly named **Hibiscus Trader** in 1990, before reverting to **Sletter** later in 1990. She was purchased by Kaalbye Shipping at Singapore in September 1992. (*Barry J. Eagles Collection*)

The 1979 Gdansk built B345 type *Zarina III* was photographed outbound from Durban on 10 October 2005. Delivered to Ecuador on 1 December 1979, she served as *Isla Floreana* until sold at the end of 1996 to Platte Steamship Company of Mauritius. Thereafter operated for three years as *Floreana*, she was then acquired by Kaalbye to trade as *Zarina III* until beached for scrapping at Alang on 19 April 2006. (*Trevor Jones*)

K&O Shipping of Panama (Kaalbye International)'s 1976 Turku built cruise ship *Olvia* in the River Mersey on 19 October 1998 preparing to enter Langton Lock, Liverpool, stern first on an ebb tide. Built for the Soviet Union as *Kareliya*, she was honoured with the name *Leonid Brezhnev* between 1982 and 1989. Purchased by Kaalbye earlier in 1998 from Black Sea Shipping Company, she was "sold east" in 2004, becoming *Starry Metropolis* in 2011. After being laid up from March 2016 she departed from Hong Kong on 4 May 2021 under tow of the tug *TC Vigour* bound for Alang where she was beached on 14 June 2021. (*Author*)

The bulk carrier **Svyatoy Georgiy**, seen in Piraeus Roads, was acquired by Aleksei Fedoricsev in 1997 and managed by Priamos Maritime of Athens until sold for breaking in 2003, the year in which Fedcom was established in Ukraine. Delivered at Muroran in 1971 as **Maria Voyazides**, she had been renamed **Vomar** in 1976 and sold in 1989 to Mayfair (Hellas) to trade as **Mayflower** until purchased by Fedoricsev. **Svyatoy Georgiy** had Ukrainian styled funnel colours, with the letters SG in yellow on a wide blue band, and had called at Mariupol in December 2003 before heading to the breakers at Gadani Beach, arriving in February 2004. (*Peter Fitzpatrick*)

Fedcom's bulk carrier **Sv.Nikolay** was photographed from New Brighton as she sailed out of Liverpool on 9 July 2011 with a cargo of scrap metal. The letters FAM painted on her funnel presumably stand for Fedoricsev Aleksei Monaco. Delivered at Osaka in 1983 to Sir Y.K.Pao of Hong Kong as **World Oak**, after 1986 she had five other names concluding with **Sorbona** when operated by Priamos Maritime from 2006 to 2009. As **Sv.Nikolay** she was thereafter managed from Ukraine by Fedcom until sold for scrap late in 2012. She was beached at Alang on 3 January 2013. (*Author*)

UKRAINE SHIPS JOINT VENTURES

The 1966 Szczecin built B44 type *Amfitriti* in Singapore Roads on 2 May 1991 during a voyage from Dalian to Ravenna. Launched as *Aleksey Tolstoy*, she was delivered into the management of Black Sea Shipping Company as *Millerovo*. Transferred in 1990 to Ukraine's Transblasco joint venture and renamed *Amfitriti*, following a final voyage from Ashdod to India in September 1992, she arrived off Alang on 23 October 1992 to be scrapped. (*Ian Shiffman*)

Black Sea Shipping Company's Kherson built Dnepr type *Hurst* in Singapore Roads on 18 June 1997. Delivered to the Soviet Union as *Grigoriy Petrenko* on 30 June 1980, this was one of a number of ships briefly managed in the mid-1990s by V.Ships' Silver Line of London. Several of the Silver Line managed ships were named after England footballers, in this case Geoff Hurst who famously scored a hat-trick in the 1966 World Cup final. Having idled at Singapore from 25 December 1996, *Hurst* was renamed *Lucy* later in 1997, by then managed by Ukline, one of BLASCO's new subsidiary companies. *Lucy* arrived off Alang for scrapping on 9 September 1998. (*Nigel Jones*)

The 1982 Szczecin built B181 type *Pearce*, named by manager Silver Line after the footballer Stuart Pearce, was photographed arriving at Felixstowe in May 1998 with yellow and blue funnel colours, thought to reflect her Ukraine ownership. With a container capacity of 994 TEU, she had been delivered to Palm Line of London as *Lagos Palm* and was purchased by the Soviet Union in 1986. Renamed *Boris Andreyev*, she was operated by Black Sea Shipping Company and in 1996 managed by V. Ships (Cyprus) Ltd. Soon sold to Spanish buyers, she then traded as *Nieves B.* until renamed *Ahraf B.* in 2009. She was reported at Port Said on 29 August 2009 and, as *Sahra*, arrived off Alang for scrap on 23 September 2009. (*Author's Collection*)

RUSSIAN SHIPS NORTHERN SHIPPING COMPANY

Northern Shipping Company's 1968 Vyborg built **Bakaritsa** outbound in Garston Channel on 12 March 1994 following discharge of a cargo of tincal ore from Bandirma in Turkey. In 1995 she was transferred to Unimar management to trade as **Daria I** until detained at Piraeus from 26 November 1996 and sent to Aliaga for scrapping in June 1998. (*Author*)

Sovetskiy Moryak, built at Nikolayev in 1971, preparing to enter Langton Lock, Liverpool, stern first on the morning ebb tide of 29 July 1997 on arrival from Thessaloniki. On 25 June 1998 she sailed from her home port of Archangel for Alexandria where she was subsequently handed over to Romalex Marine and renamed **Ashraf R**. Following a return voyage to Alexandria, arriving there from Odessa on 18 August 1998, she sailed for Galatz to load a cargo of beechwood for Egypt. Unfortunately her cargo shifted, causing her to founder in the Sea of Marmara off Ambarli port on 17 November 1998, but with no loss of life. (*Author*)

The 1988 Gdansk built *Inzhener Plavinskiy*, which was lengthened by a Chinese shipyard in January 2008, is seen entering Gladstone Lock, Liverpool, on 20 August 2011, probably from her home port of Archangel. Reflagged to Malta between 1997 and 2016, she was one of the Project B352 series of eight timber carriers built by Stocznia Gdanska between 1986 and 1991. A further eight vessels of this type were constructed in Malta to the order of Sudoimport. The final port of call of *Inzhener Plavinskiy* was Haifa in Israel, from where she sailed on 25 January 2021 bound for Aliaga in Turkey where she was beached for scrapping on 9 February 2021. (*Author*)

The 1973 built *Mikhail Cheremnykh* approaching Gladstone Lock on 1 September 2000 on arrival at Liverpool from her home port of Archangel. A total of twelve packaged timber carriers of this type were built for the Soviet Union by Finnish shipyards in 1972/74. *Mikhail Cheremnykh* was one of five built by Hollming O/Y at Rauma. In 2009, she was sold to Murr Shipping of Lebanon and renamed *Spiridon II*, as which she was converted by 2011 for use as a livestock carrier and continues to trade as such, since 2018 under the flag of Togo. (*Author*)

The 1976 Vyborg built *Pioner Estonii* entering Gladstone Lock, Liverpool, on 19 February 2006. She was one of twenty-four Project 1590P (*Pioner Moskvy*) type general cargo ships constructed for the Soviet Union between 1973 and 1981, again to a design developed by the Central Design Bureau "Baltsudoproekt". Two others of the type, *Heidenau* and *Rabenau*, were delivered to East Germany in 1979 (but returned to Northern Shipping Company in 1993) followed in 1981 by *Jugo Navigator* to owners based at Belgrade, Yugoslavia. *Pioner Estonii*, last reported as due into Mundra in India on 2 June 2010, was beached at Mumbai on 19 June with work commencing on 4 August 2010. (*Author*)

Konstantin Yuon, built at Turku in 1974, sailing from Eastham on 14 August 1997. Sold to Syria in February 2007, she was renamed *Mr. Ahmad* and, when resold to Lebanese buyers in April 2008, was given the name *Andelin*. She was beached at Aliaga for scrapping on 6 April 2013. (*Author*)

When *Kungurles* arrived at Eastham on 6 August 1992 from her home port of Archangel, her funnel had still not been painted in the post-Soviet colours of Northern Shipping Company. It is therefore assumed that an early sale was planned. In 1994 she was transferred to Unimar management to trade as *Uniprogress* until sold at Piraeus in 1996 to Syria and renamed *Al Hareth*. She was reportedly beached for scrapping at Mumbai on 19 January 2003. (*Author*)

RUSSIAN SHIPS
MURMANSK SHIPPING COMPANY

Murmansk Shipping Company's 1981 Warnemünde built **Pavel Vavilov** preparing to enter Gladstone Lock, Liverpool, on 12 August 2006 on arrival from the Far East with a cargo of steel. In 2008 she was lengthened and stripped of all cargo handling gear, allowing the vessel to operate more efficiently until sold for scrap to India in 2017. **Pavel Vavilov** was beached at Alang on 7 July 2017. (*Author*)

Vasya Korobko was a Pioner type ship built at Rostock in 1970 for the Soviet Union, operated on its behalf by Murmansk Shipping Company. She was seen in the Manchester Ship Canal at Eastham, outbound on 6 April 1995 following discharge of a cargo of bagged PVC pellets at Ellesmere Port. **Vasya Korobko** finally arrived at Alang for scrapping on 18 October 1997. (*Author*)

RUSSIAN SHIPS
WHITE SEA & ONEGA SHIPPING CO

The 1966 Turku built **Morskoy-1**, owned by White Sea & Onega Shipping Company of St.Petersburg, passing Marina di Ravenna inbound on 12 August 1996. In 2004 she was transferred to Volga Trans Marine of Astrakhan and her last reported movement was bound for Anzali in the southern Caspian Sea, arriving on 28 May 2013. In February 2016, her owners became Ing-Trans Shipping Agency of Sevastopol but her current situation is not known. (*Author*)

White Sea & Onega Shipping Company's 1978 Komarno (Czechoslovakia) built **Volgo-Balt 213** inbound for Ravenna on 17

May 2002. The Petrozadovsk based White Sea and Onega, previously part of North-Western river shipping company, had entered into foreign trading from 1965. It was established on 1 July 1940 to transport cargoes and passengers along the White Sea- Baltic Sea Canal in the north of Russia. In 2007, together with numerous sister ships, **Volgo-Balt 213** was transferred to an owner in Astrakhan which employed Istanbul based managers. Since 2017 she has been registered in Panama. (*Author*)

RUSSIAN SHIPS
BALTIC SHIPPING COMPANY

The Rauma, Finland, built **Kapitan Gastello** sailing from Eastham on the evening of 25 August 1992. She was delivered to the Soviet Union's Northern Shipping Company on 21 July 1967 but was transferred to Baltic Shipping Company in 1975. Sold in 1994 to Riamar of Tartous, Syria, she then traded as **Nina** until February 1996 when renamed **Rossa**. Resold in April 1996 to Turkish buyers and renamed **Aksel**, from mid 1997 she traded as **Alkan** until sold in 1999 to Yucedadi Shipping of Tunisia and renamed **Sunset**. She was last reported sailing from Djibouti for Aden on 18 July 2001; she did not return to the Mediterranean and is assumed to have been scrapped. (*Author*)

Lomonosovo, another of the twenty-four **Kotlasles** type timber carriers built at Rauma between 1962 and 1971, was delivered to the Soviet Union on 24 April 1968 for operation by Baltic Shipping Company. Twenty-four similar ships were constructed at Uusikaupunki (Nystad) over the same period. In addition, ten ships of the similar **Ladogales** type were built at Helsinki, plus twelve at Turku, between 1964 and 1970. Their prototypes were the twelve engines aft ships of the **Igarkales** type constructed at Turku between 1961 and 1964 (see **Izhevskles** on page 40). **Lomonosovo** was photographed in the River Mersey approaching Garston Docks on 18 May 1993 with a cargo of tincal ore from Bandirma. Also sold in 1994 to Syria, she traded as **Muhieddine IV** until 1999, then as **Rwala** until beached at Alang for scrapping on 25 August 2001. (*Author*)

The 1967 Leningrad built **Novaya Ladoga** approaching Garston on 3 February 1996 from Bandirma, it is thought on her last loaded voyage for Baltic Shipping Company. Soon transferred to Balthellas, she was renamed **Iris** at Riga on 4 April 1996 and then **Olga** shortly before sailing from Ipswich on 16 August 1996 bound for Greece. Following a final voyage from Southampton on 18 December 1998 for Turkey, **Olga** arrived off Aliaga on 18 January 1999 for breaking. **Novaya Ladoga** was a Project 596 type of which a total of 41 ships were built between 1962 and 1968, twenty-two by the A.Zhdanov shipyard at Leningrad and nineteen at Vyborg. In subsequent years, sixteen of these ships were converted into research vessels. (*Author*)

Professor Nikolay Baranskiy arriving at Birkenhead on 19 August 1992 with a cargo of rice bran from Kakinada. She was the last of twelve Irkutsk type ships built at Warnemünde between 1967 and 1970. These were followed between 1970 and 1972 by a second series of fourteen ships, each given a 60-ton derrick. On 28 July 1996, following a voyage from Havana, the vessel was arrested at Québec City and sold at auction to the locally based Unispeed Group. Renamed *Phoenician Trader*, it is thought managed by Ordina Shipmanagement of Cyprus with possible Russian or Ukrainian interests, she returned to Liverpool in July 1998 to load a break-bulk cargo for Apapa/Lagos. After loading a similar cargo at Ilichevsk, sailing on 18 December 1998, she proceeded from Apapa to Calcutta for breaking, being beached there on 10 May 1999. (*Author*)

Baltic Shipping Company's Warnemünde built improved Irkutsk type *Olga Ulyanova*, which was delivered to Baltic Shipping Company in September 1970, discharging a cargo of AFS from India in Huskisson 3 Branch Dock, Liverpool, on 16 January 1994. In mid 1996 she was transferred to Euroshipping A/O, also of St.Petersburg. Following a final voyage from Spain to India, she was beached for scrapping at Alang on 29 April 1998. (*Author*)

RUSSIAN SHIPS
NOVOROSSIYSK SHIPPING CO

The 1985 Spanish built ore/bulk/oil carrier *Kapitan Spivak* sailing from Liverpool, stern first out of Langton Lock, on 17 June 2000. One of a series of six similar ships delivered to Ultramar Shipping of New York as *Maureen*, she and three of her sisters were purchased by the Soviet Union in 1989 for operation by Novorossisyk Shipping Company ("Novoship"). The final two ships were purchased by Novoship in 1992. Sold at Piraeus in September 2003 to Halkidon Shipping (Southern Shipping & Finance) of Piraeus, *Kapitan Spivak* then traded as *Olympia* until resold in August 2005 to buyers in Qinhuangdao and renamed *Hebei Victory*, as which she was beached at Chittagong for scrapping on 6 November 2009. (*Author*)

The twin screw *Novorossiysk*, one of three Project 16075 type ro/ro ships constructed at St.Petersburg between 1992 and 1996, was photographed passing Terneuzen, inbound for Antwerp, on 28 March 2002 to load cargo for Apapa/Lagos. Originally intended for operation by Baltic Shipping Company ("BSC") as *Kirishi*, she was delivered as *Novorossiysk* to Novoship in August 1994. The lead ship *Kronshtadt* was operated by BSC until 1996, then managed from Cyprus by Interorient Marine Services until sold to Grimaldi in 1999. In July 2004 *Novorossiysk* was sold to Norwegian Car Carriers (Eidsiva Rederi of Oslo) for conversion into the car carrier *Vinni*. She was beached at Alang on 31 January 2014 for breaking. The final ship *Sochi* was also sold to Norwegian Car Carriers in 2005 and scrapped in 2014. (*Simon Olsen*)

Vladimir Vysotskiy, built at Rijeka in 1988, sailing from Eastham on 24 February 2007. Between 1984 and 1989 a total of twenty-seven "Josip Broz Tito" type tankers were built for the Soviet Union by two Yugoslav shipyards, at Rijeka and Split. Sold in April 2008 to North Eastern Shipping of Petropavlovsk-Kamchatskiy, her manager later became Vostokbunker of Slavyanka (Primorsky Krai). On 21 January 2017 *Vladimir Vysotskiy* arrived at Ningde in China from Slavyanka for intended demolition at Fu'An on the Bai Ma river. The scrapyard however resold the vessel and from September 2018 she operated as *Zhong Yuan 18*. On 10 July 2021, under the shortened name of *Zhong*, she anchored off Chattogram (formerly Chittagong) to await breaking. (Author)

RUSSIAN SHIPS OTHER COMPANIES

The nominally C.I.S. owned and Sovcomflot controlled 1993 Vegesack built CS2700 type **Bremen Senator**, seen arriving at Felixstowe on 18 July 1999 to load for the east coast of the United States. She was one of the ten containerships which had been ordered specifically to lease to Senator Linie and Deutsche Seereederei for use in a joint service with Cho Yang. Managed by Unicom of Limassol, she was chartered out during 2003 to India as **SCI Vaibhav** and then sold to Mediterranean Shipping Company to trade as **MSC Mandy**. (*Simon Olsen*)

The Mercur type container ship **Mor U.K.**, managed by Delphic Shipping Company of Athens, was photographed off Gladstone Lock inbound for Seaforth Dock, Liverpool, on 8 August 1998. She was one of three containerships transferred by Baltic Shipping Company to the Cypriot flag in 1994 to operate as the Morline transatlantic service. Built at Warnemünde in 1979 for the Soviet Union as **Nadezhda Obukhova**, she was given the name **Essex** in 2000 and chartered out in 2002 as **MSC Sumatra**. In 2004 she was purchased by Mediterranean Shipping Company, sailing as **MSC Immacolata** until beached for scrapping at Alang on 30 December 2009. (*Author*)

Pan Oceanic Ship Management Company of London's Malta flagged **Baltic Guard** vacating her berth for a container ship at Greenock's Ocean Terminal on 2 May 1997 while discharging a cargo of sugar cane for the Tate & Lyle refinery, which by then had ceased to use James Watt Dock and soon closed, on 27 August 1997. A second series Irkutsk type ship, built at Warnemünde in 1972 as **Boris Zhemchuzhin** for the Soviet Union, she had been operated by Baltic Shipping Company until November 1996. On completion of discharge, **Baltic Guard** sailed to Falmouth for orders, departing on 9 July for Ukraine from where she made her way to Yangon in Myanmar before being sold for scrap at Calcutta, arriving on 14 January 1998. (*Graham Thursby*)

The 1966 Rostock built *Ivan Serebryakov* outbound in Alfred Basin, Birkenhead, on 19 February 1996. Since 1991, many private shipping enterprises have been created in Russia, albeit often registering their ships under flags of convenience. Thus, Black Sea Shipping Company's 1966 built *Severodvinsk* was acquired in 1992 by clients of SA Shipping of St. Petersburg and flagged out to Belize, managed from Cyprus, as *Ivan Silver*. In December 1995 she was renamed *Ivan Serebryakov* and transferred to the Cambodia flag. In mid 1997 she made her way to Singapore, then to Mumbai, before being beached at Alang for scrapping on 11 December 1997. (*Author*)

Volgotanker of Astrakhan's "Hummingbird" type chemical/oil products tanker *Inzhener Lupichev* approaching Langton Lock, Liverpool, on 15 April 2006, probably with a cargo of molasses. Built at Volgograd (formerly Stalingrad) in 1997, she was managed from Limassol in Cyprus by Sampratrans Shipping Ltd. In 2012 she was sold to Trans-Flot JSC of Novorossiysk and renamed *Marshal Tukhachevskiy* and in 2017 resold to E.E. Rubakova (Staksel Co. Ltd.) of Samara and registered at Taganrog. She continues to be based at Astrakhan on the Volga River in southern Russia. (*Author*)

Duglas T.O.O. of St.Petersburg's *Iosif Sichinava* berthing at Garston on 2 April 1999. She was built in 1970 at the Krasnoye Sormovo shipyard, one of the oldest shipbuilders in Russia, located in Nizhny Novgorod (formerly Gorkiy). Delivered to North-Western River Shipping Company as *Petr Zalomov*, she was traded by Duglas as *Iosif Sichinava* from 1998 until 2006 when sold to Ukraine's Odessa Link Ltd. In 2007 she was resold to Turkish buyers and renamed *Aliberr*, as which she was beached for scrapping at Aliaga on 21 October 2010. North-Western state river shipping company, formed in 1923, became JSC North-Western Shipping Company in 1992. In 2020 it was absorbed by Volga Shipping JSC. (*Author*)

Khazar Star-2 was one of four ships with Omskiy names built at Oltenita in Romania, which between 2001 and 2005 were managed by Palmali Shipping of Istanbul on behalf of Ennec Ltd (Enisei-Neva Company) of St.Petersburg. Seen loading grain at Port-Saint-Louis-du-Rhône on 19 February 2004, she was the former 1983 built *Omskiy-112* which between 1994 and 2002, when named *Ob*, had been managed from St.Petersburg by Neva Company. From 2005, when renamed *Prudential*, her manager became River Med Trading of Rostov-on-Don, then from 2013, as *Pioneer*, by Black Sea & Baltic Shipping Company of St.Petersburg. She continues to trade in the Black Sea area. (*Author*)

The 1967 Turku built *Lidiya* at anchor off Limassol on 8 September 1999, reportedly to be renamed *Lilian*. Built for the Soviet Union as *Turku*, she was one of seven similar ships transferred in 1995 by Baltic Shipping Company to the Russian Federation owned Altex Shipping of St.Petersburg. Soon transiting the Suez Canal to Jeddah, on 16 May 2001 she was reported sailing from Fujairah, still as *Lidiya*, but was sold in 2002 and renamed *Erica*, owned by Jiu Li Shuen Trading of Kaohsiung. In October 2003 this company had purchased another ship, the 1974 built tanker *Mare Altum*, also naming her *Erica*. It therefore seems likely that the former *Lidiya* was scrapped in 2003. (*Author*)

The 1967 Komsomolsk built diesel-electric powered *Navarin*, which in 1995 had been purchased from Murmansk Shipping Company by the locally based Joint Stock Company "AIF", discharging a cargo of aluminium at Liverpool on 4 December 1998. *Navarin*, a sister ship to *Pavel Ponomaryev* (see page 34), was soon sent to India for breaking, arriving off Alang on 17 July 1999. "AIF", which registered its ships in Russia, closed in 2000 following the sale of *Olenegorsk* (see back cover) and *Sasha Borodulin*.(*Author*)

The Moscow based AO Sovfracht's *Ozersk* in Alfred Basin, outbound from Birkenhead on 11 March 1999, during a voyage from Baltimore to St.Petersburg. A semi-container "Mercator" type, the former *Walter Ulbricht* (see page 36) built at Warnemünde in 1974, originally with a 60-ton heavy lift derrick, she had served Baltic Shipping Company as *Priozersk* from 1992 until 1997 when transferred to AO Sovfracht to become *Ozersk*, as which she finally arrived for scrapping at Alang on 15 December 2000. (*Author*)

The 1984 Wismar built *Motovskiy Zaliv*, a "Kristall II" type fish carrier delivered to the Soviet Union for operation by Sevryba (after 1992 by Sevrybkholodflot) of Murmansk, is seen berthed at St.Petersburg on 1 July 2000, the photograph probably taken from a visiting cruise ship. In 2004 *Motovskiy Zaliv* was transferred to Murmantransflot of St.Petersburg to trade as *San Diego*, from 2009 operating as a refrigerated general cargo ship, until beached for scrapping at Chattogram on 20 April 2018. A total of twenty-seven ships of this type were built in East Germany between 1983 and 1993. (*John Wiltshire*)

Luktrans of Novorossiysk's 1995 St.Petersburg built, project 15966 type, tanker *Urai* entering Port de Bouc harbour, near Marseille-Fos, on 27 April 2002 heading for Lavéra oil terminal. Luktrans was established in 1996 with three Cypriot flag tankers named *Langepas*, *Urai* and *Kogalym*. *Urai* had a varied history, having been launched as *Belanja* for Belships of Norway but traded, presumably on time charter to Sovcomflot, as *Pavlovsk*. In 2005, when renamed *Pacific Ambassador*, her nominal owner became Khazar Star Two Shipping Co. Ltd. Sold back to Norway in 2007, she traded as *Chem Marigold* until sold to Turkey in 2009, from 2012 as *Nireas*. She was beached at Alang on 8 December 2018 as *Pro*. (*Author*)

Atlantic Ro/Ro Carriers (ARRC)'s 1992 Warnemünde built, LoRo18-II type, *Atlantic Navigator* arriving at Eastham from Houston on 9 May 2015. Delivered to Baltic Shipping Company as *Kovrov*, she had been arrested at Tahiti in December 1995 due to a claim arising from the bankruptcy of Baltic Line which had operated the previously Finnish owned 1973 built ferry *Ilyich*. Sold at auction late 1996 to Russian clients of manager Oceanbulk Maritime of Athens, *Kovrov* had traded as *Thorsriver* until 2000, and then as *Lykes Energizer*, before being acquired by ARRC in 2004. *Atlantic Navigator* was beached at Chittagong on 15 January 2017 for breaking. (*Author*)

Mys Zhelaniya is a good example of a modern multi purpose ship purchased second-hand by Russian interests. Built at Shanghai 2008 as *Beluga Generation*, following several changes of name concluding with *BBC Ontario*, she was purchased by Transstroy LLC of Archangelsk in November 2019. *Mys Zhelaniya* was photographed in the River Dvina in October 2020. (*Vitaliy Vashutkin*)

The 1991 Harlingen built, Spliethoff "Gracht A" type *Tambey*, the former *Ankergracht*, owned by TK Nord Project LLC ("TKNP") since 2016, is seen berthed at Archangelsk in February 2020. For the purpose of a time charter between March 2012 and October 2013, she had traded as *Tasman Sky*. Six of the seven ships of this type, built for Spliethoff by Frisian Welgelegen at Harlingen in 1990/91, were purchased by Russian companies between 2012 and 2017. (*Vitaliy Vashutkin*)

TKNP's's Bilbao built **RZK Constanta** berthed at Archangelsk on 5 November 2015, with Northern Shipping Company's 1992 Malta built **Inzhener Trubin** astern. **RZK Constanta** is TKNP's oldest ship, and the only one built for the Soviet Union, constructed in Spain between 1989 and 1991 as **Vysokogorsk** for FESCO and acquired by TKNP in 2016 following two years with Rezkozan Impex of Constantza. (*Evgeniy Zhelezov*)

The St.Petersburg registered **Volgo-Don 155**, built at Navashino in 1972 for the Volgo-Don Shipping Company of the Soviet Union, passing along the Svir River in the north-east of the Leningrad region on 2 May 2021. Svir is the largest river flowing into Lake Ladoga, connecting it with Lake Onega, thus uniting the two largest lakes in Europe. Peter the Great's vision to build a waterway linking the Volga River to the Baltic Sea was realised in the early 19th century. In order to accommodate larger vessels, the Volga-Baltic Waterway was rebuilt in the mid-20th century, when the Rybinsk Reservoir was constructed at the northern end of the Volga. Since 1994, **Volgo-Don 155**, which was originally registered at Yeysk, a port on the Taganrog Gulf of the Sea of Azov, has been owned by JSC Volga Shipping of Nizhny Novgorod, the sixth-largest city in Russia, on the Volga River. (*Anatoly Rudkov*)

RUSSIAN SHIPS
JOINT VENTURES

Nasia, operated by Balthellas of Greece, berthed in Garston Docks on 10 September 1999. Another of the Project 596M type, constructed at Vyborg in 1968, she was operated as *Plesetsk* by Northern Shipping Company until mid 1998. On the transfer of her management to Balthellas she was initially named *Katia* but was renamed *Nasia* early in 1999. Following a voyage from Söderhamn in Sweden to Jeddah in August 2000 she was beached for scrapping at Alang on 23 September 2000. (*Author*)

The 1968 Turku built *Tanya 1* outbound from Garston on 13 June 1997 bound for Hernösand in Sweden to load cargo for Patras in Greece. Her management had only recently been transferred to Balthellas from Northern Shipping Company which had operated her as *Koporye*. In 1999 she was renamed *Valia* as which, in January 2002, she sailed from Mudanya in Turkey to the Persian Gulf and Kandla, from there on to Somalia where she was sold to Rose Marine Shipping of Dubai. Renamed *Aziza*, she sailed from Berbera to trade in the area until beached for scrapping at Mumbai on 16 February 2004. (*Author*)

The 1968 built *Daria I*, formerly Northern Shipping Company's *Bakaritsa*, off Piraeus under arrest on 23 December 1997. In 1995 she had been transferred to Unimar management to trade as *Daria I* but was detained at Piraeus from 26 November 1996 and sent to Aliaga for breaking in June 1998. Although another of the Vyborg built second series of Project 596M type ships constructed between 1965 and 1972, as was the case with *Vytegra* (see page 42) her design was that of the Leningrad built *Vytegrales* type, of which *Novaya Ladoga* (see page 66) was an example. (*Nigel Jones*)

Uniarch, formerly Northern Shipping Company's *Pamir*, built at Vyborg in 1970, transiting the River Loire near Saint Nazaire on 22 May 1991, soon after being transferred at Piraeus in February 1991 into the management of Unimar. In 1995 she was sold to Ali Sahyouni of Lattakia, Syria, to trade as *Bassel* until beached for scrapping at Alang on 8 October 2000. (*Patrick Blaise*)

Balt-Med Shipping Company, a joint venture with Gourdomichalis Maritime of Piraeus, was formed in 1992 to manage five of Baltic Shipping Company's general cargo ships, the oldest being the 1965 Warnemünde built *Vereya*, renamed *Ifigenia*. Photographed southbound in the Suez Canal, passing Port Tewfik, on 6 April 1993 on a voyage from Novorossiysk to Vietnam, it was at that time reported that she was to be renamed *Georgios* but she instead proceeded to Chittagong, arriving there on 14 June 1994 to be scrapped, still named *Ifigenia*. (*Bertil Palm - Simon Olsen Collection*)

Black Sea Shipping Company's Gdansk built B44 type **Boris Gorbatov**, which was delivered to the Soviet Union in April 1967, southbound in the Suez Canal on 25 April 1996 on her last voyage. Following discharge she anchored off Alang on 25 May and was beached on 2 June to be scrapped. (*Gerhard Fiebiger*)

Also photographed southbound passing Port Tewfik, on 28 April 1996, the Gdansk built B40 type **Nikolay Kremlyanskiy** had been delivered to the Soviet Union in November 1968. Following discharge of a cargo at Manila in November 1996 she idled for some months before being transferred into the management of Ocean Agencies Ltd. of London and Sudoservice of Odessa, briefly to trade as **Irene 2** until beached at Alang on 4 October 1997 for breaking. (*Gerhard Fiebiger*)

Baltic Shipping Company's 1971 Warnemünde built **Valerian Kuybyshev** southbound in the Suez Canal passing Port Tewfik on 21 June 1995 during a voyage from Muuga in Estonia to Bombay. In 1996 she was transferred into the management of Euroshipping A/O of St.Petersburg, from mid 1997 trading as **Euroshipping 6** until beached for scrapping at Alang on 17 January 1999. (*Author*)

Novorossiysk Shipping Company's **Stoletiye Parizhskoy Kommuny** was photographed passing Port Tewfik, on 27 May 1996. The last of the Project 1563 or **Slavyansk** type (see page 45), built at Kherson in 1971, the Soviet Union had transferred her from the Black Sea Shipping Company in 1989. Following a voyage in August 1998 from Argentina to Constantza she proceeded to Chittagong, where she was beached for scrapping on 19 November 1998. (*Author*)

Irina GA., managed by Unimar Maritime Services of Piraeus, northbound passing Port Tewfik on 17 June 1994. Another Project 596M type, built at Vyborg in 1967, she was operated as *Kuloy* by Northern Shipping Company until 1993. In September 1995 she passed to the Syrian owner Ibrahim Mostafa Shehadeh of Lattakia, and later to Ahmad Toumen of Tartous, trading as *Noor Alddine* until beached for scrapping at Mumbai on 29 October 2001. (*Author*)

Black Sea Shipping Company's 1986 Warnemünde built LoRo 18 type *Korsun-Shevchenkovskiy* entering the Suez Canal northbound at Port Tewfik on 30 May 1996 during a voyage from Madras to Marina di Carrara. Soon transferred into the management of V Ships and renamed *Houston*, she was frequently renamed for charters, notably as *African Sky* between 2002 and 2007. Sold in 2008 to South Korea for conversion into a vehicle carrier, she emerged as *Oriental Elf* and briefly traded as *OS Yangon* from February 2012 until arriving at Jingjiang on 18 December 2012 for breaking. (*Author*)

GEORGIAN SHIPS

Ocean Shipping Company of Georgia's 1988 Split built, "Brodosplit 505" type, tanker **St. Mary** passing Ellesmere Port in the Manchester Ship Canal, outbound from Stanlow, on 18 September 2004. She had been delivered to the Soviet Union as **Akademik Uznadze** for operation by Georgian Shipping Company ("GESCO"). Her name was shortened to **Uznadze** in 1994 but she remained in Georgia's fleet when reconstituted in 2000. Then renamed **St. Mary**, she was retained in the fleet when it was privatised in 2005, trading as **Aral Wind** until mid 2009, when the fleet was dissolved. Purchased by Fortune Tanker JSC of Primorskiy Kray and renamed **Zaral**, she made her way to eastern Russia but was soon resold to Chinese interests. From April 2010 until August 2015, when beached at Chittagong for scrapping, she traded as **Yu Fu**. (*Author*)

GESCO's 1967 Nantes built ferry **Memed Abashidze** at anchor off Istanbul on 16 March 1998. Built as **Dragon** for Normandy Ferries (P&O Group until 1985, then Townsend Thoresen until 1987, when it became P&O European Ferries), she was renamed **Ionic Ferry** in 1986. Sold in 1992 to Cadet Shipping of Malta, she then took the names **Viscountess M.** and **Charm M.** before becoming the Georgian **Memed Abashidze** in 1997. Sold to Access Ferries of Piraeus at the end of 1999, she sailed as **Millennium Express II** until suffering a fire in her engine room off the Strofades Islands on 2 March 2002. There abandoned, the fire was extinguished four days later and she was towed to Eleusis Bay. Declared a constructive total loss, in April 2003 she was towed to Aliaga under the abbreviated name of **Millenium** for demolition. (*P. Tabagua*)

BALTIC STATES - ESTONIA

The 1975 Szczecin built B46 type **Emel I** passing Ellesmere Port on the Manchester Ship Canal on 26 May 1997. Delivered to the Soviet Union as **Aleksandr Vinokurov** for operation by Estonia, her name was changed to **Tamsalu** by ESCO in 1992. From 1994, although nominally owned by the Russian domiciled Dashanov & Co. Ltd. and from 1995 by Merktrans Shipping of Tallinn, she traded as **Emel 1**, indicating an underlying continued beneficial ownership by ESCO, then trading as Eesti Merelaevandus AS. At the end of 1997, after once again briefly sailing as **Tamsalu**, she was sold to Filsa Shipping International of Singapore and flagged in Panama. Renamed **Sea Endurance**, she thereafter traded east of Suez until beached for scrapping at Alang on 23 June 2001. (*Author*)

Two views of ESCO's 1963 Rostock built **Ristna** approaching Langton Lock, Liverpool, on 25 May 1993. One of the **Povenets** type (see page 35) delivered to the Soviet Union for operation by Estonia, she retained her original name on transfer to the Estonian flag in 1992. In 1994, she was sold to Russian interests and renamed **Lena**, managed by JSC North-Western Shipping Company of St.Petersburg. Then trading east of Suez, **Lena** was beached at Calcutta on 4 October 1995 for breaking. (*Author*)

Tootsi, the former **Vilyany**, built at Rostock in 1964, approaching Liverpool on 21 May 1993 when employed on Eesti Merelaevandus AS ("ESCO"), E.M.E.L. liner service from the eastern Mediterranean Sea. As with sister ship **Ristna**, she was delivered to the Soviet Union for operation by Estonia, retained her original name on transfer to the Estonian flag in 1992 and was sold to Russian interests in 1994. Renamed **Lada**, she briefly traded in the Far East before being beached to be scrapped at Calcutta on 29 September 1995.(*Author*)

81

Latvian Shipping Company's ("LSC")'s 1975 Finland built 4207 type ro/ro *Inzenieris Kreilis* arriving at Felixstowe on 2 June 1996. She had been delivered to the Soviet Union as *Inzhener Kreylis* for operation by Latvia with her name changed to *Inzenieris Kreilis* on transfer to the Latvian flag in 1991. Following three years managed by the ADG Group of Riga, she was beached for scrapping at Aliaga on 27 February 2002. Ten ships of this type were built by Hollming at Rauma for the Soviet Union in two series of five, the first between 1973 and 1975, of which *Inzhener Kreylis* was the last to be delivered, and the second in 1976/77. *Inzhener Kreylis* was for many years a frequent visitor to Ellesmere Port on the Manchester Ship Canal. (*Gary Goodman*)

The 1983 Leningrad built ro/ro *Juris Avots* was photographed from Étang de Gloria near Port-Saint-Louis-du-Rhône as she departed from Marseille-Fos for Algiers on 25 January 2003. She had been delivered to the Soviet Union as *Yuriy Avot* for operation by LSC with her name changed to *Juris Avots* on transfer to the Latvian state in 1991. From 2002 she was on time charter to Leif Hoegh's French subsidiary Cetam SAS which served the cross-Mediterranean short sea market. In March 2004 *Juris Avots* sailed for Sevastopol and was renamed *Telo*, returning to service in the Mediterranean until sent to Alang for breaking, being beached there on 8 July 2009. (*Author*)

LSC's 1986 Gdynia built B365 type reefer *Belgoroda* arriving at Heysham on 23 June 1996 from Larnaca in Cyprus with a cargo of potatoes. She had been delivered to the Soviet Union as *Byelgorod* for operation by LSC with her name changed to *Belgoroda* on transfer to the Latvian state in 1992. Following several months idle at Riga in 2003, she was sold into the management of the local company Aquaship Ltd. and her name shortened to *Belgorod*. Having sailed from Riga to Chittagong via Durban, she was beached on 18 June 2004 for breaking. (*Author*)

The 1965 Rostock built **Stepans Halturins**, which had been delivered to the Soviet Union as **Stepan Khalturin**, arriving at Mostyn, North Wales, on 10 September 1994 from Constantza via Belfast with a part cargo of bagged PVC pellets. On 13 May 1996, when berthed at Waterford in Ireland, she was sold to Syria and renamed **Rima M.** before loading a cargo for Alexandria. In mid 1997 she was renamed **Wendy M.**, sailing from Ghent on 4 July for Turkey, but was next seen in Cawsand Bay near Plymouth on 16 August 1997 as **Rima M**. She continued to trade under that name until the end of 1999 when renamed **Riad M**. Unfortunately, on 26 June 2000, she suffered an engine room fire and was towed to Arwad Island, eventually making her way to nearby Tartous on 20 October 2000. There she was repaired, sold and placed under the flag of Sao Tome and Principe as **Dana**, sailing in March 2001 for Jeddah. Sadly, during a voyage from Somalia to Dammam in August 2001, she suffered a fire in her accommodation and sank off the coast of Dhofar, Oman. (*Author*)

LSC's 1984 Kherson built tanker **Asari** passing Portishead, outbound from Portbury Dock, early in the morning of 8 April 2007 following discharge of a cargo of molasses. One of five Project 15965 or **Dmitriy Medvedyev** type tankers developed by the Central Design Bureau "Izumrud" and built between 1983 and 1986, she was delivered to the Soviet Union as **Georgiy Kholostyakov** for operation by Latvian Shipping Company. Soon after being renamed **Asari** in 1992, she was "flagged out" to Cyprus. Sold in 2008 to Dubai buyers, she traded as **Artemis** until beached for scrapping at Alang on 1 September 2011. (*Author*)

The 1985 Rijeka built tanker **Kemeri** was photographed from an overtaking P&O ferry from Hull when inbound for Rotterdam from New York on 31 May 2000. Another of the of twenty-seven "Josip Broz Tito" type tankers built between 1984 and 1989 (see **Vladimir Vysotskiy** on page 68), she was delivered to the Soviet Union as **Yuliy Danishevskiy** for operation by Latvian Shipping Company, her name was changed to **Kemeri** on transfer to the Latvian flag in 1991. She was beached for breaking at Alang on 21 June 2009. (*Author*)

BALTIC STATES - LITHUANIA

Lithuanian Shipping Company ("LISCO")'s 1971 Rauma built **Marijampolė** inbound in the Garston Channel on 14 July 1996. Launched as **Kavgolovo**, she was delivered to the Soviet Union as **Kapsukas** with her name changed to **Marijampolė** on transfer to the Lithuanian state in 1991. In 1998 she was sold to Dnieper Bureau of Shipping Ltd. of Kherson and renamed **Pegasus**. Early in 2000 she was transferred to Poseidon Shipping before being sold late in 2001 to Regal Co. Ltd. of Nakhodka, Russia, and renamed **Argus**. Then sailing for the Far East, it seems managed from Hong Kong, she was eventually sold to Chinese breakers at Zhangjiagang on 30 April 2009. (*Author*)

LISCO's 1979 Kherson built project 1592 type bulk carrier **Kapitonas Domeika** under tow outbound in Birkenhead's West Float on 14 April 2006. She had been delivered to the Soviet Union as **Kapitan Vavilov** for operation by Murmansk Shipping Company until 1992. Then transferred to Lithuania, her name was changed to **Kapitonas Vavilov** and in 1995 to **Kapitonas Domeika**. Sold in 2007 to the Turkish subsidiary of Sea Pioneer Ltd of Beckenham, Kent, she traded as **ICJ Venture** until sold to Chinese breakers, finally arriving at Zhangjiagang on 13 February 2011. (*Author*)

LISCO's 1976 Oltenita (Romania) built project 740/2B ("Young Partisan") type **Marat Kozlov** departing from Great Yarmouth for Klaipeda on 11 December 1991. She had been transferred to the Lithuanian state early in 1991 and was soon to be renamed **Nida**. During 2000, in order to trade more profitably, her cargo gear was removed, she was reflagged to Cambodia with nominal ownership by Eko International of Delaware, United States, and was managed from Singapore by SembCorp Marine. Renamed **Santa Nikolas** in 2002, she sailed from Chioggia on 11 November 2002 bound for Chalkis in Greece where she remained until departing on 29 April 2004 bound for Lebanon. In October 2003 she was sold to Al Safa Maritime Services of Tartous, Syria, and renamed **Oday H**. Managed by the locally based Akram Shipping, she was further renamed **Lady Rana** in 2005 and then traded on until scrapped at Aliaga, where she was beached on 2 June 2009. (*Gary Goodman*)